A Learning Journal:

thoughts on teaching Foundation

Chameleon Press

Kansas City, MO
Copyright 2020 Hugh Merrill
ISBN: 978-0-9990222-8-3
designed by: Jeanette Powers

A Learning Journal:
thoughts on teaching Foundation

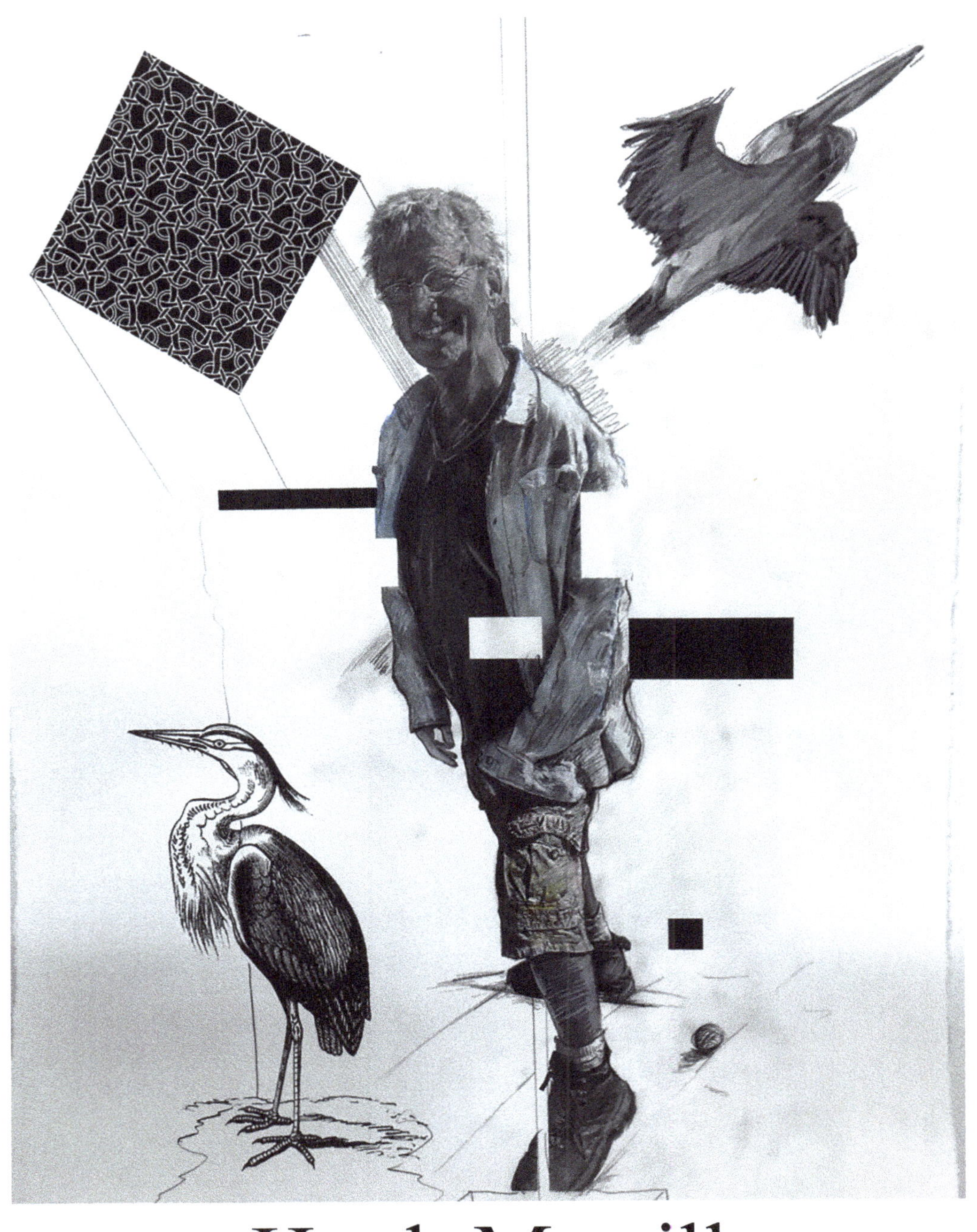

Hugh Merrill

Acknowledgments

I have been teaching for over 46 years most of that time at the Kansas City Art Institute in Painting, Printmaking, Social Practice, and Foundation. I have also been director of Chameleon Arts and Youth Development for over 30 years working with homeless children and teens in the Family Court System. These teaching experiences are the underlying resource for this text. There are also several colleagues who have greatly impacted my attitude on teaching in the Kansas City Art Institute Foundation Department. I want to thank Russel Ferguson, Steve Whitacre, Jim Sajovic, Carl Kurtz, and Eleanor Erskine, for their support deep and meaningful discussions on teaching art and education. I want to thank Jeanette Powers, Sharon Eiker and the "family" of creative poets and writers that I love working with, amazing folks all. I also want to thank all the students I have taught over four decades and so deeply appreciate all that they have taught me. Especially the students in the fall semester of 2018 on whom this text is based:

Adrian Powers, Ashli Owens, Bri Armstrong, Christina Wells, Daisy Sieben, Diada Jones, Esther Lee, Hannah Kosmas, Jacob Turley, Jada Jacobs, James Bell, Jessica Cook Lizzy Zirkel, Nina Gale, Noah Anthony, Sarah Stne, Theodore Morris III, Tyler James.

Note on this publication:

I did not start out to publish this learning journal as a book. I simply wanted to keep a day by day record of what my students in the Foundation Department at the Kansas City Art Institute were learning. As the semester ended, I went over my notes and decided to put them into shape and that shape turned out to be this publication to my surprise. The photos I shot of the student's work were done simply from my phone. When I was shooting I had no plans to take professional quality photos. The photos are what they are.

Table of Contents

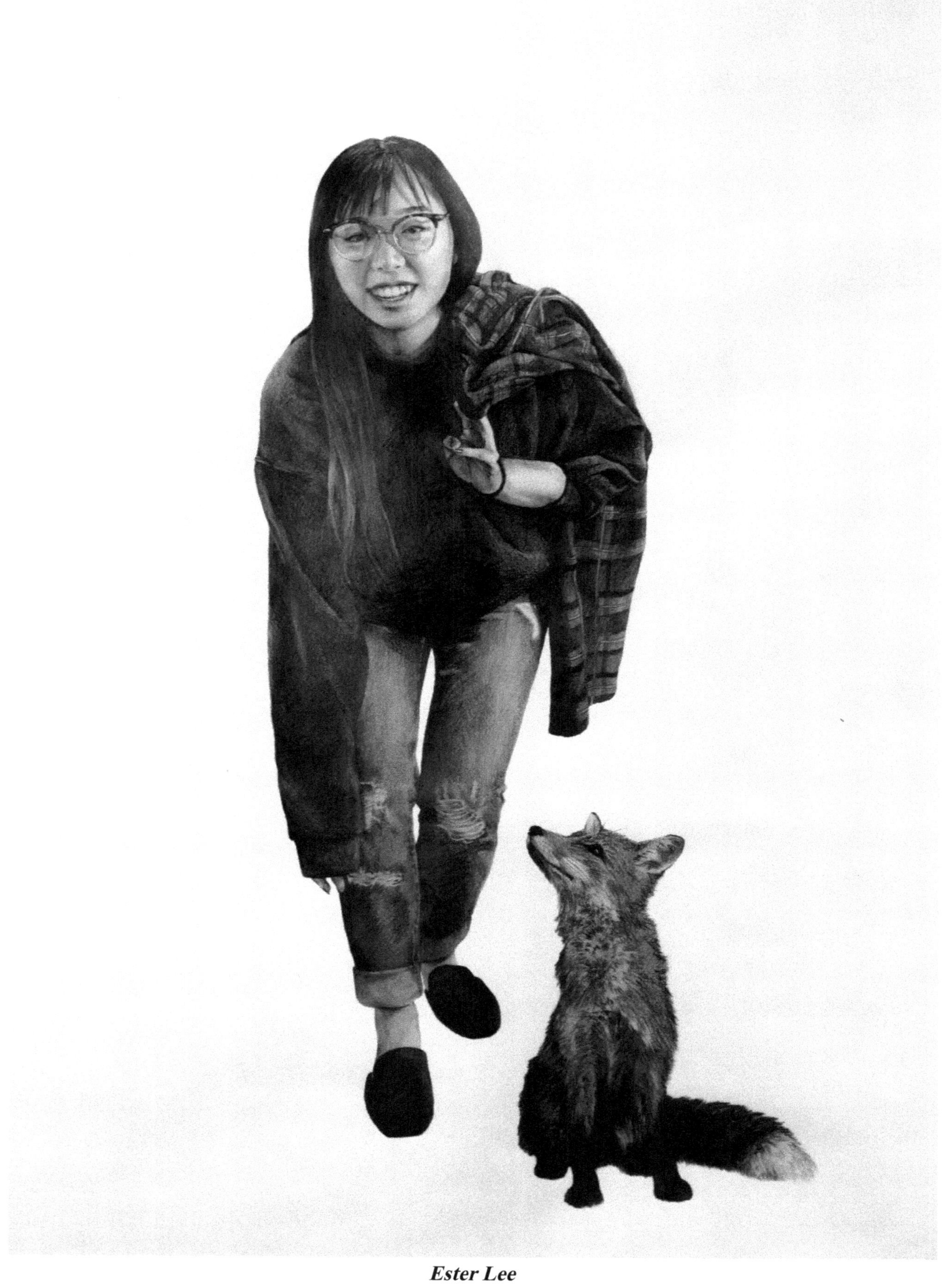

Ester Lee

My process is grounded in making, research, content, discernment, discussion then remaking/rethinking.

There are some things that can be taught in a consistent manner, such as the way to use a tool or a system of tools, as well as how to tie a shoe or read a clock. But how do we teach art? Are there steps that proceed in a linear fashion from level one to level two? What should be taught first?

As educators, can we teach talent, insight or brilliance? Should art schools only teach the most talented students and ignore the rest? Is it even **Art** that needs to be taught, or are there other layers of making, thought and creativity that are worthwhile to a broader group of learners? Artists-educators struggle with these questions.

Yes, skills can be taught. However, there are no sets of specific tools that teach people to become artists. When students learn about color, line, design, composition or form, they are encountering the building blocks of visual thinking. Perhaps these steps even direct the student to become an artist. Yet, it is not these skills, but **knowledge** that is necessary to become an artist. Knowledge encompasses an understanding of complex visual, conceptual, social and poetic relationships. These are the forces articulated through fundamental visual skills that come to play in studio practice; in making art and design, knowledge matters most.

Dietmar Winkler, an artist and graphic designer, once commented to me, "teaching is for skill and education is for knowledge." He used this framework while a professor at the Kansas City Art Institute.

Dietmar Winkler saw that knowledge is a complex series of overlapping relationships that move us away from the obvious and towards a deeper understanding of both self and culture. He saw that this could be a process presented to students, as a territory in which they could learn and create deeply.

No set of classes and skills will transform a group of interested students into artists.   However, there is a process for providing students with experience, research and information, in combination with dedicated studio practice, that will lead to deeper creative thought and penetrating socio-cultural investigation. This system is knowledge based, and does not depend on talent and skill alone.

Instead, **it is the knowledge expressed through craft, exploration of materials, and studio practice that matters. The iterative process is grounded in making, then research, content discernment, discussion and remaking-rethinking.** It is a process that engages students in complex layers to approach creativity, culture, the concept of self and the use of materials as a connected ecosystem. This is an educational approach that goes beyond teaching the fundamentals of art based in formal and thoughtful Bauhaus principles. It is a process of thinking and making that is of value to a broad set of students from all disciplines. It is a process of exploration for artists and designers and for those in the system that will find their contributions to society outside the framework of the arts.   It is a deeply thoughtful investigation into creative thinking, materials, self and cultural analysis.

Who are We Teaching?

Over the past five decades, student interest in arts programming have significantly branched out. The art world and its creative focus expanded in response to the technology for graphic design, photography, film, and animation becoming increasingly accessible to the non-arts public.   The growth of arts programs in high schools, community colleges and Universities have increased the opportunity for more students to experiment in visual culture and art making. The opening of society to communities that were left out, such as women, persons of color, and LGBTQ+ folks, to name but three, have brought new diverse perspectives to art making, design and creativity. The number of students applying to arts colleges and taking arts programming may not be increasing but the various access points for entering the arts has grown and diversified. In short, students are not only painters, designers, craft people and sculptors. They do not come to school from a mono-culture based in patriarchal European norms. They are diverse, yet quickly connected through technology and social media. (There is much written on this generation of students and their connection to technology and their changing educational behaviors and interests but these issue goes beyond the scope of this publication.)

Conceptual and social practice concerns ask artist to move beyond materials and traditional disciplines. Students come to art school who will work as developers of inner city or rural communities. They will follow relational aesthetic process to change the behavior of society and address the worlds most pressing social and ecological problems.

 These realities underpin the fierce competition for students to sustain the numerous arts programs in colleges, Universities and private art institutions. As a result, art schools are attempting to broaden the pool of potential applicants. Embracing students that may not be grounded in traditional artistic processes and interests means that each studio class has students with widely varied interest and expectations for attending arts programming. These dynamics put further pressure on what should be taught and how that information should be approached.

This more diverse pool of students will continue to be interested in the traditional modes of artistic production and investigation. It also will produce many students that will earn the BFA degree and go on to work in modes never seen before and use their degrees in un-expected ways. In fact, it is my guess that most BFA students will make their living doing something beyond studio practice and outside the traditional territory of the visual arts. During my forty years at KCAI, I have seen many students use this education to become better teachers, entrepreneurs, and corporate workers. They join creative ventures outside design and the arts. I strongly believe there are values to receiving a BFA that go beyond training artists and crafts people. The process of education must significantly benefit all the students brought on campus. For these reasons, educational practices must evolve.

When I came to KCAI in 1976, there were six majors: painting, printmaking, sculpture, ceramics, design, and fiber. Today we have thirteen available majors, including creative writing, product design, illustration, animation, entrepreneurial arts, and social practice.   There are even more across the teaching spectrum in other arts institutions.

Think of the range of interest the students bring: from making children's books to museum work; figurative painting to conceptual work; industrial design to animation; community art to sculptural forms. In addition, ponder all of the beautiful crafts. Further, think of the means of artistic production: the simple drawing made with a pencil, to complex fabrication with computerized routers, lases, looms, 3d printers, and the organization of communities into a single arts action.

Professional opportunities have grown, while disciplines and majors have increased. We work in both traditional and emerging materials, with the invention of new uses for art. The spectrum of the arts has significantly expanded.

The community attending art school has also grown to more truly reflect the rich diversity of our nation. In 1968, when I attended the Maryland Institute College of Art, the students were by far white and male. Today, students come from a diverse range of ethnic backgrounds, gender identities, and economic situations. Each student brings new approaches, outlooks, communities and aesthetics to the institutions. All of these realities have significantly altered the educational system. The best of the art schools have accepted this challenge and made productive changes to meet the needs of their students.

Process to Deepen the Learning Opportunities

The first year of art college is the critical Foundations year. Foundations programs try to bring a set of experiences, skills and processes to the students that cut across disciplines and are valuable in all future areas of study. The educational problems becomes more complex, as students enter a creative world where artists are less likely to stay in one discipline. More artists will wander freely through and between categorical areas of study. Most departments at KCAI seek to be interdisciplinary and allow students wide latitude in defining the scope of printmaking, fiber, painting, ceramics, and sculpture. You are as likely to have a video artist doing performance in painting or sculpture as in photography or film. The educational problem is how to combine breadth of connections between disciplines with depth of individual studio practice. Here, I believe that the traditional Foundational educational structure, which focuses on formal issues of art and design, needs to be coupled with creative thinking and an emphasis on conceptual connections to cultural and society. The student must learn to connect disparate ideas, processes, aesthetics, and disciplines. They need a knowledge-based education with strong conceptual practice that goes beyond fundamental skills of visual literacy.

Students come to "art school" with an interest in many ideas. However, many come with limited visual literacy and are fixated on manga, anime, graphic novels and related pop cultural references. They have learned to draw hair like Team Rocket's Jessie, James, and Meowth and eyes the size of ostrich eggs on cute anime faces. They hope to flock to illustration and animation departments to follow their narrow teen driven narratives.
The Foundation education must be designed to take them beyond their narrow primary thinking and reality. It must challenge them to move out of their enclosure of limited culture knowledge.

At the end of the year's exploration, students must enter their selected areas of study. Foundations is meant to ensure that they approach this journey with a deeper and more expansive knowledge of self, the creative process, materials, technology and most importantly, culture. They often do move into illustration and animation, but with a much richer creative and visual understanding. The journey they have taken to move beyond primary thinking will enrich their participation in these important disciplines. This is the reason I employ this educational direction with my classes: we seek to balance fundamental visual exploration and broader issues of creative thinking, and concept.

Learning is not about what the students want to do, but what they need to do to make imaginative and insightful work and to think creatively. They need to learn a process to create work and explore concepts from a territory beyond their primary reality.

The self is determined in relation to our cultural exposure. We are not blood and tissue; we are makers and thinkers shaped by our use and understanding of cultural images, ideas and the signs surrounding us.

> *The artist swims in an ocean of culture. From this sea of ideas and images, we are nourished to create more cultural substance and make more art in all its varied forms.*

The Foundation education is a process to take the student beyond their primary thinking and expose them to deeper and more complex currents of art and thought. Art is not about self-expression but about cultural manipulation and articulation. The realm of the new is built firmly on the present and on the past. Each generation of artists, designers, directors and creators will add to the depth of our collective human history.

While self-expression is common and perhaps universal, achieving a BFA degree is not about self- expression. It is instead about expanding the sense of self in relation to culture, bringing the student-artist to the edge of their cultural knowledge, and guiding them past the edge of their preconceived notions. At this edge, is the world of invention, creative exploration, and life. The self is expanded and investigated not by repeating and mimicking, not by demonstrating what we already know, but by expanding into a territory of ideas, images and culture that we do not understand or recognize easily. It is at this edge of individual knowledge and familiarity that the student begins to become creative, insightful, and truly self-expressive. This is where the really hard work begins for the student.

Formal Artistic Practice

Some things do not change: for example, how we see color and color relationships, as aptly described on a color wheel. Color has been technically described by artists Anni and Josef Albers and Johannes Itten. Their work creates a Foundational vocabulary for discussing and understanding color. Like the qualities of color, there are other fundamentals that all artist-students need to know: qualities of line, contour, gesture, shading, visual points of entrance in an image, composition, letter-forms and many more. There are also the experiences with materials, like charcoal, pen, clay, fiber, and watercolor. All have unique qualities and certain conceptual and visual characteristics.

Aesthetic realities include developing a knowledge of craft and seeing what makes a great ceramic Japanese Tea cup great. Students must discern why an etching, figure painting or fiber work is held up as visually meaningful. Each form and discipline comes with its own aesthetic values, vocabulary, and history. Students must grasp these values and aesthetics as they begin their journey.

Yet, these standards or fundamental skills are not the central focus of art making and educating the next generation of artists. These fundamentals are essential to perception for an artist but they need to be part of a larger system of conceptual, cultural, social, semiotic, and experiential knowledge that teaches creativity, context and lateral thinking. The student needs to learn how to visually research an assignment, both for visual aesthetic content and for social poetic content. They need to understand how meaning is created and how meaning is communicated from contemporary painting to advertisements. They need to understand that meaning and content already exists in the visual communications they see and manipulate. Content and meaning do not arise from self-expression and the articulation of an individual's internal world. Many of my best students come in believing content is a personal narrative. Through the assignments and experiences, they learn that content is more complex and exists in the context of visual communication.

It is fundamental to the process of learning for students to become a cultural sponge. They must absorb the artistic explorations of the past and present to build their own expression.

T.S Eliot says *"immature poets imitate and mature poets steal."*

The process I apply is grounded in making, supported by visual research, semiotic investigation of content, discernment, discussion and studio practice by remaking-rethinking. Then doing it all over again.

There is nothing new or groundbreaking in the assignments I give to students. Rather, it is the overlapping of the fundamental assignment with layers of cultural, social and lateral thinking that are important. The learning outcome goes beyond the studio work to involve conceptual thinking and research. Many others have accomplished this task before me.

Theatre of learning

The learning theatre is a performance in an educational setting by the faculty turning the classroom into theatre space. The lectures are non-linear and tie together many subjects and information areas. Moving from art to diversity, appropriation, Disney animations, literature, consumerism, comics and back to art and making. Humor and acting skills are used in making presentations. Each days' class is partly a theatrical experience. Reading poetry prior to drawing from the model, drawing to music, teaching movement prior to gestural drawing are but a few examples.

As with a play the audience has the opportunity to see and experience deeper meaning within the actions on stage, there is more there than the simple words and basic story. The theatre of learning goes beyond the teaching of a skill or a process. It goes beyond the industrial classroom setting.

The industrial metaphor for the classroom is one in which all the students are treated as learning units and are fed information, and assignments to be completed. The assignments are evaluated in relation to a set standard. The industrial classroom does not evaluate the learning of the students but address the correct answer. Simple math is a good example and if you add 1+1 and get 3 your answer is wrong. Here the system works very well.

If the course is a creative workshop or artist studio experience the assignment is not simply evaluated by the student's answer. The final work turned in or reviewed is meant to develop creativity, expand curiosity, and to have the student take greater responsibility for learning and conceptualizing. The artwork produced is only a component of the evaluation process. The student is learning to sift through the faculty dialogue to discover deeper avenues for investigation and meaning. They are asked to go beyond the completion of the assignment. Through developing intellectual curiosity and self-guided research, based on faculty lectures/performances, they are to extend their own knowledge. They are to become knowledge creation organisms. This ability is the most important factor in evaluation. Are they learning?

In my drawing courses I do not assess solely by talent, looking for who draws the best. I ask who learns the most. Both skill and learning capacity, are part of the evaluation process.

In my creative writing course, if the student hears me discuss HOWL by Ginsberg and other Beat poets and knows little about them but is interested enough to look up Howl on their own, they are working as an A student. They are working like a professional artist. If on the other hand they do an excellent job on the assignment make a beautiful and interesting image/text work and wait for me to explain who the Beats are and why Howl is important then they are B students. It is the invisible that matters as much as the thing made.

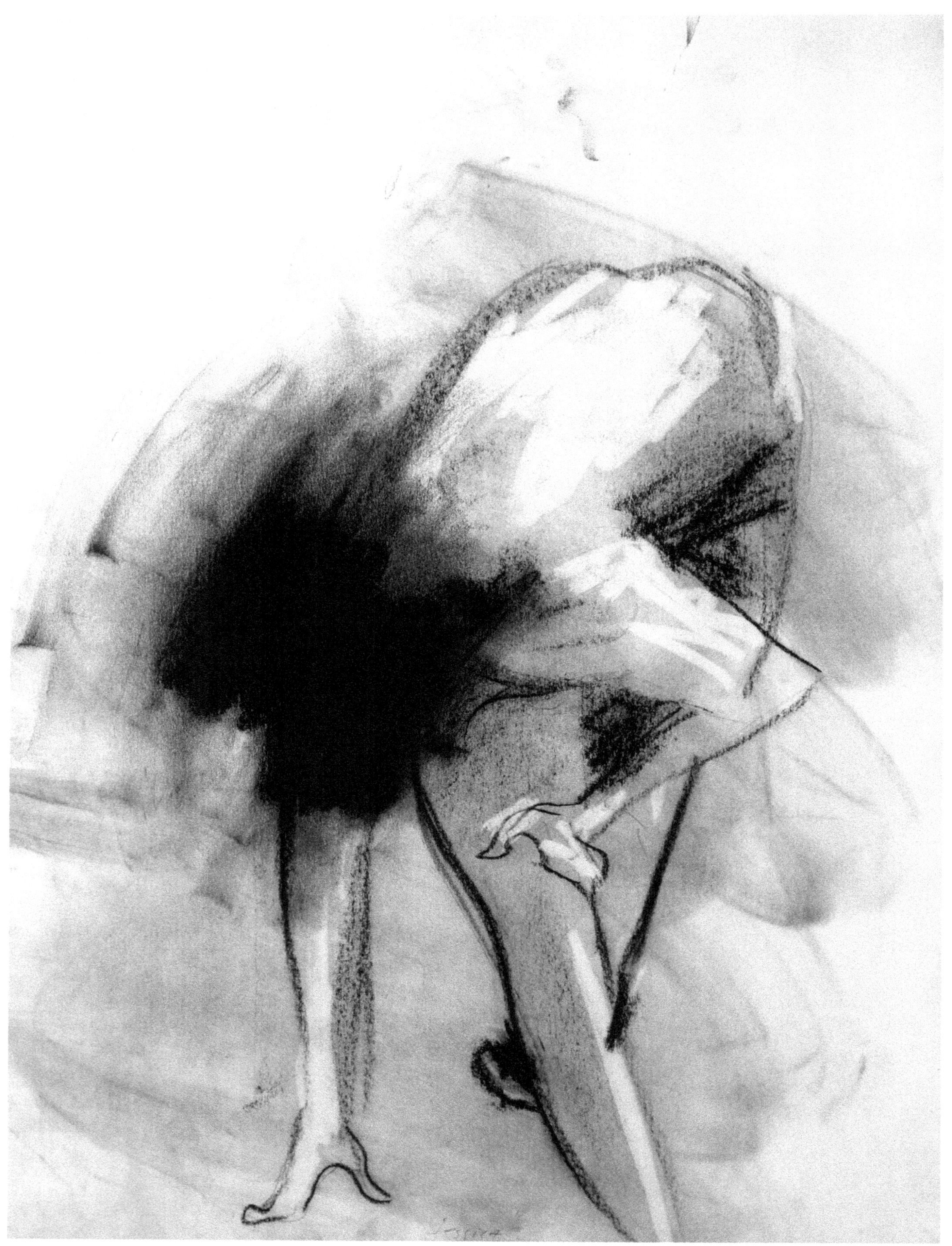

Studio drawing response

Introduction to the Studio Community and Creative Thinking Process

In working with first year Foundation students, the primary goal is to develop the studio or class community by presenting a series of non-judgmental activities that are not based in talent. This is a significant departure from the traditional competitive environment known as the classroom.

For example, if we were to ask students to draw a self-portrait, we would effectively separate the perceptual drawing students from those whose skills center in graphic design, sculpture, fiber and so on. Listen to a group of senior high school students brag about the colleges they have gotten into, their test scores, or the amount of scholarship offers they have received. They define their friends by levels of talent, where one's identity is closely tied to skill: Tenesha is in theatre, Jose is great with math, and Leslie is a basketball player. They enter the studio with pre-considered restrictions and prejudices concerning what they can and cannot accomplish. They are often worried about what they do not know or are not good at. If they fail to make a good drawing in the first class it is not about the drawing experience but about the impairment to their confidence as a learner. They say "I can't draw" as a form of self-defense; they seldom say I am going to learn to draw.

We ask students to risk and take chances, but all too often the studio community which fosters a sense of safety is not successfully developed. Students will find they are forcefully critiqued on their works in an attempt to build critical thinking skills. Does a forceful critique early in the student's studio experience build their confidence to take risks? Or does it achieve the opposite: timidity. Further, the student is often asked to speak about their work and others when they have yet to develop the vocabulary and principal studio experiences to formally describe a work and delve into its visual content. They tend to talk about what the work makes them think of, how it stimulates their memory and not about the visual or content possibilities.

Students often lack basic cultural and aesthetic knowledge. Understanding of the depth and commitment necessary for successful studio practice takes nurturing. It is the aim of this process to develop these skills, rather than dismiss the students as wanting. The class can quickly be divided between those that are more mature and have more experience and those lacking in maturity and creative experiences. It is important to develop the early classes, so that the more mature are not separated from the less sophisticated students, but are used as part of the learning experience to develop everyone's skills. Building a strong learning community is the first step.

Process

The first week of studio focuses on a series of workshop experiences to build community, vocabulary, demonstrate good studio practice, attention, and lateral thinking. The exercises are set up to have a degree of comedy, playful embarrassment, social interaction and encourage storytelling.

The students coming into a new program, in this case Foundation at KCAI, have just entered college and endured a week of sitting in chairs in large groups and being the objects of various lectures. On the first day of studio, I hardly introduce myself and never go over the outline of the course. I do not talk at them, continuing to separate them as students and me as faculty/authority. We go to work on a visual project based in mapping and information graphics. This is the first task.

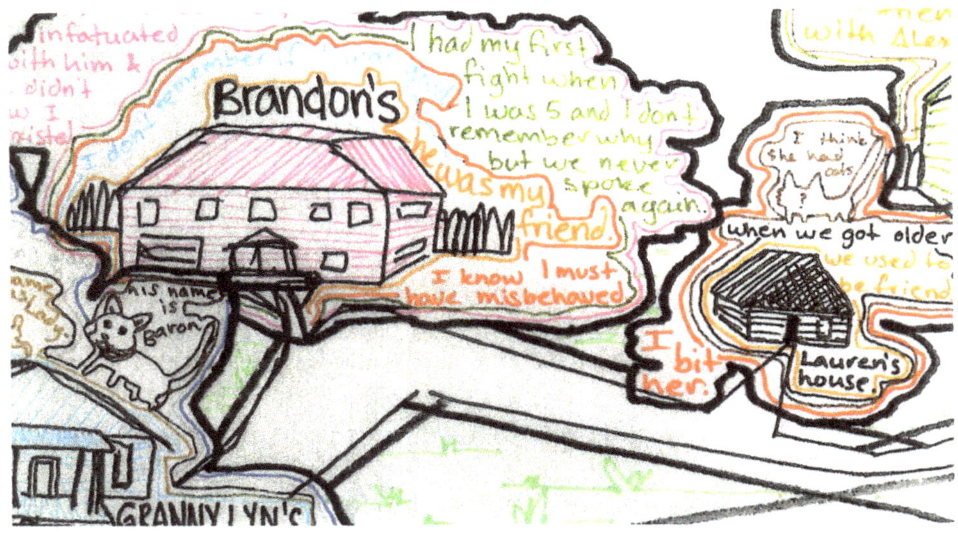

Draw a map of your primary neighborhood and mark on it all the places you were bad. Add other prompts, such as: who were your friends, where were you good, where did the dogs live, and more------------

The students use 18x24 inch drawing paper for this exercise. I provide crayons, markers, scissors, construction paper, tape and glue sticks. I dump all this material out on a central table and tell them to help themselves. These materials stop the student from relying on pencil or pen which is their default mark making tool. The very existence of construction paper and glue suggests collage without having to use the word. It hints at making their maps three dimensional and layered. Pushpins suggest that the map can be assembled on the wall. I allow them to discover these possibilities.

One or more students will say they have finished their maps in about half an hour, I will show them to the class and then add new prompts and point out the importance of creative continuation: *when you are finished how do you start again? how do you take the project further?* I provide new prompts, such as *where was the closest liquor store to your home? Where was the closest cow?* (Some students are from the inner city and some are from rural Kansas). *Make a list of your friends and where did they live? Which one was the first one you got into a fight or broke up with? Who had a pet that died, where were you embarrassed by a parent*, and so on. They go back to work.

It is only after about 60 minutes of work that I call everyone back together and I go over primary thinking, explaining that our goal is to go beyond what we know and are "good" at. That we are starting the process to attain a college degree, the Bachelor of Fine Arts and that the course is not about what you want to do or even self-expression but about learning and moving into unfamiliar territories of investigation. We are searching for new and unexpected visual relations. Let's not repeat what we know. This method breaks down working from skill and claiming a territory/identity based on talent and past successes. These points will be reinforced often during the next 5 weeks to firmly establish a deeper understanding of our goals and how to get there.

Then we continue to develop and extend the information on our maps. We end the day with a look at the work, but it is not time for a critical analysis or for story-telling. More in depth discussion will be taken up the next day. For the homework, they are to continue to add information to the maps by adding new prompts. I explain that they should talk to each other, take ideas from others to add to their maps. I point out that the act of borrowing or building on others ideas and prompts is good—it is not stealing. We are here to help and stimulate each other. It is not a competition and not about "it" being mine. I discuss ownership and creativity, learning and continuation.

For homework, I ask them to look up Edward Tufte online and see the difference between information graphics and "posters." I tell them to set up a resource folder on their Google drive to collect visual resource information: they are to make a new folder titled Tufte and pull into it from the web information graphics that interest them. They ask simple questions and want specific answers such as how many images should I download? I suggest about 10 or perhaps 100. This will be an on- going homework format for the rest of the semester. For every studio assignment where the students work with materials; drawing, painting, collage and such, they will have a conceptual research assignment. Here, they view and collect the work of other artists and visual information. This process quickly expands their aesthetic baseline of images, possibilities and visual ideas. This image research builds curiosity and interest in other artists and ideas into their studio practice. The process moves the student away from self-expression centered on ownership and connects them to a progression of history and ideas.

Day Two

The following day, we begin in the digital studio looking at the Edward Tufte collection of information graphics. I lecture on their relation to our maps. How the maps are information graphics. We also look up ancient maps and I discuss how these are not maps alone, but graphic and text stories of travel and journals of events.

We return to our studio (class space) and each student tells the story of their childhood based on their maps.

This activity moves the students into presentations and public discussion and storytelling. The subject is something they know a great deal about and even the most quiet and shy student is able to build trust and confidence in presenting their map to the class. More importantly, they are building a strong community by telling in depth the story of who they are. When they tell about times they failed or were embarrassed, connections between students with like experiences arise. All the students are vulnerable and a little embarrassed and it is this openness that creates a connected community.

Where is the Box and How Do You Get Out?

On the completion of the map assignment, we use the next several classes to discuss and consider creativity. Again, this is not a talent-based series of exercises but is meant to provide the students with a process to consider future assignments and an examination of what it is to think creatively. In a student's primary thinking pattern, they are given an assignment and they quickly choose a direction and begin. They seldom use creative or lateral thinking processes to come up with multiple ideas to consider prior to engaging in the studio activity.

Can creativity be taught? Yes, absolutely. The process is similar to teaching any other thought process. Learning tools for creativity may not make a person an artist, but they can change the way a person approaches a problematic situation and help them come to a new decision.

We start with the question draw a bird house.

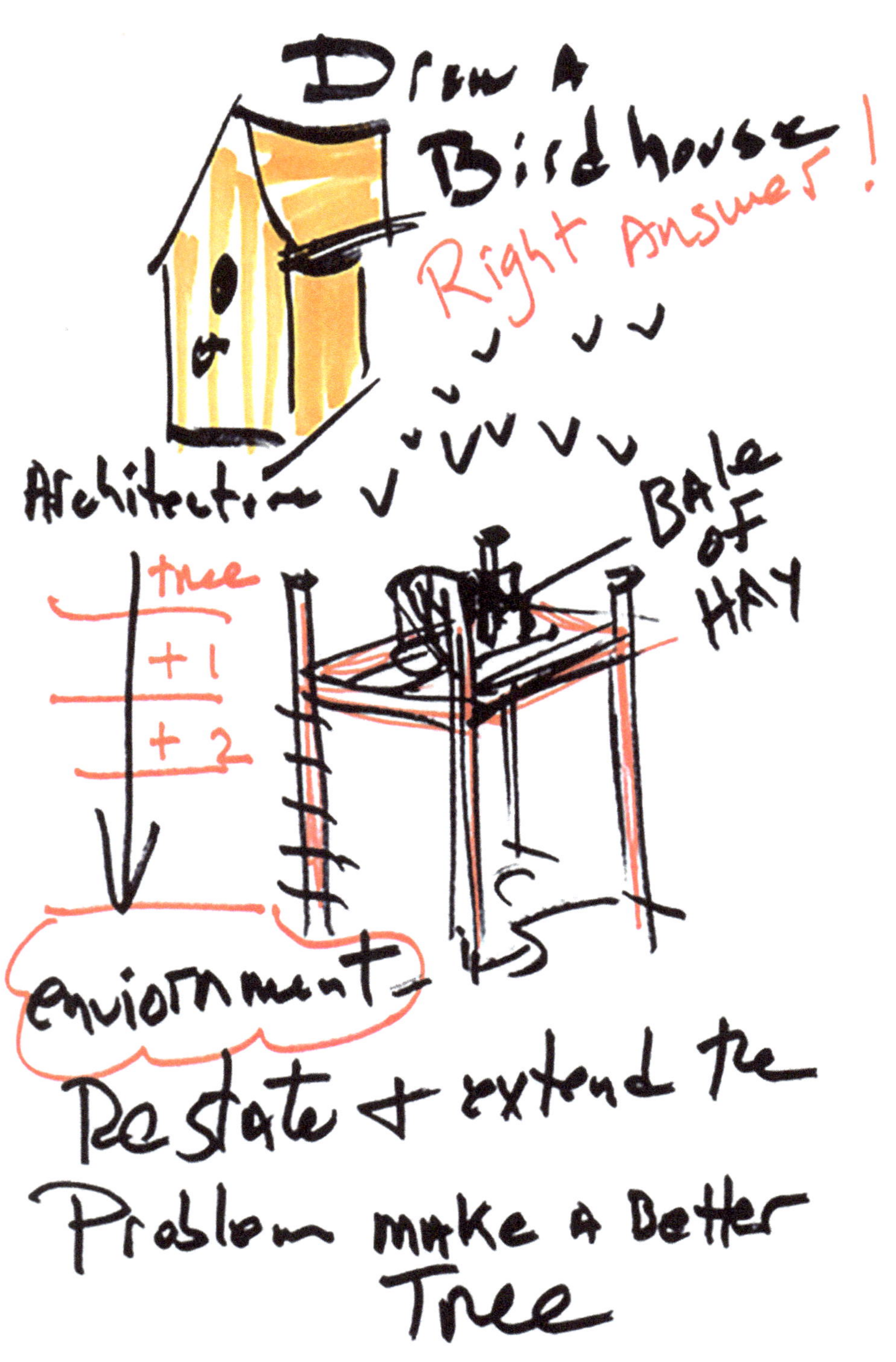
Draw A Birdhouse !
Right Answer!
Architecture
tree
+ 1
+ 2
enviornment
BALE OF HAY
Restate + extend the Problem make a Better Tree

Assignment I: Draw a Birdhouse

This exercise teaches that the correct answer is seldom the creative and innovative answer. I ask the group to draw a birdhouse. I have done this exercise with social workers, grad students, art students at all levels and from all disciplinary backgrounds. Inevitably the students draw a simple birdhouse with a hole for a door and a perch. Someone usually draws a nest in a tree. I have asked what led them to think of a nest in the tree instead of a birdhouse. A typical response is that they thought of the birdhouse first, then the tree, and then elected to draw the tree. This is the *right of first refusal*, which is a door to the creative process. By refusing to use the first answer, even though you know it is correct, you open up to alternative possibilities. Going from the first answer, to ask for a second, third, or fourth response forces the person to continue to think about and redefine the question. This is the first step in basic strategies for lateral-creative thinking.

First refusal means not accepting your first answer, even if you think it is correct. The habit of stopping the investigation or thinking process, simply because you have the right answer, is what prevents new ideas. In fact, the moment you have the correct answer, it is time to immediately ask "What else is a birdhouse?" or "What else could it be?"

For many years at the Kansas City Art Institute, the sculpture department gave students the assignment of building a birdhouse. The class became a wood shop project with the students constructing elaborate birdhouses: split levels, castles, and Frank Lloyd Wright influenced structures. One student built this: he dug holes and cemented four 4'x4' ten-foot-tall posts into the ground, creating the outline of a rectangle. Then he built a platform eight feet off the ground and added a ladder so he could climb onto the platform and drill holes in the upper section of the 4'x4' posts to insert tree limbs to act as perches.

He placed a large bale of hay on the platform, and buried two galvanized buckets in the hay, one with bird food and one with water. The contraption was situated in a field on campus near a line of old trees. While no birds cared to move into the other well-crafted birdhouses, hundreds of birds flocked to this one. They built nests in the nearby trees with the straw from the bale of hay, supported by a continuous supply of birdseed and water. After about a week, the lower portion of the campus felt like the Hitchcock movie *The Birds,* and the mess they made led to the school asking that the piece be removed, which the artist did with a smile.

The young man who facilitated this habitat was Russell Ferguson, who has been the Chair of the Foundation Department at the Kansas City Art Institute. I asked Russell how he came up with the idea.   Like almost everyone else, he thought of the standard birdhouse and put that idea aside. Other architectural alternatives came to mind, which he also rejected. Once out of the spell of an architectural answer, he thought a tree was the best environment for birds. So how do you build a better tree? The answer to this question is to create a situation where safety, food, water and nesting material all come together, so the combination of elements can form an ecosystem for the birds.

The exercise reinforces the following strategies:

- Right of first refusal, do not act on your first and correct answer. Make sure to ask yourself "What else is here?"
- Do not stop with a single answer. Always come up with multiple solutions to exercises.
- Brainstorm.
- Capture and create multiple ideas rather than problem solve.
- Expand and restate the problem from "Draw a birdhouse" to "Reinterpret what a birdhouse is" or "What makes a better birdhouse?"
- To effectively extend the scope of investigation, change the language of the question.

Assignment II : What Would You Not Do to a Sheet of Paper?

I ask the class to write down what they would **not** do to a sheet of paper and let them know they have about two minutes to perform the task. I then ask them how many students have 10 answers, then 9,8,7,6,5,4, and then down to zero. One or two people will have more than a single answer, and several will have zero. I point out that the form of the question did not ask for a single answer, and again (like the birdhouse assignment) the singular response is a starting point for continued consideration.

Creativity is based on multiple possibilities and not on single answers. The American public-school system is not built on discussion and creative thinking. It is built on answering questions on standardized tests that rank achievement. The answers become important in relation to the outcome of the test only, not the deeper intellectual discourse they may foster. Art schools work to reverse the knee-jerk habits of single, simple answers, attributing one right answer to each question only. A correct answer often blocks more interesting alternatives.

I have the students read their answer(s), and they sound like this:

- I would not eat a piece of paper.
- I would not build a house out of paper.
- I did not answer the question, because there is nothing I would not do with paper.
- It was a stupid question, so I did not answer.

We examine the answers and discover several processes of reasoning that block creative thinking and participation. As soon as a reaction is written down, the person questions whether or not the answer is true. Answers are analyzed either with "accept" or "reject." The ability to suspend belief has been lost. As John Cage says: "you cannot make and analyze at the same time."

Creating a number of possibilities prior to shifting to analytical thinking is crucial. When I ask young children the question, they spout many replies, because they are seldom blocked by truth, reality, or fear of failure.

Typical answers from children include: "I would not make a dragon, or an airplane, or shoes." They automatically give multiple answers, and they laugh and enjoy the question. Children have not forgotten how to play and imagine. Adults worry about how they will be perceived or how their classmates will react to them if the question turns out to be a joke. They are nervous about being taunted by classmates. Feeling awkward and embarrassed causes a disconnection in process and participation. They make a predetermination of what a stupid question this is, so they can try to position themselves above answering it. Typically, they are wary that they are being tricked.

Adults have a fear of being wrong. School has reinforced the attitude that it is better not to participate than to be in error. Test scores and social judgments are both affected by incorrect responses, leading many to opt out if they can.

The form of the question takes the student into the vast creative space of the **land of not.** "What would you do to a piece of paper" only reinforces the obvious. "What you would not do to a piece of paper" is infinite and always creative, contradictory, and surreal. The question opens up the imagination to stimulate silly, visionary, and fantastically impossible responses.

The exercises ranging from the map, to what would I not do to a sheet of paper, and so forth, provide the student with the community, skills and experiences they will need for the upcoming assignments. The KCAI curriculum is divided into three conceptual areas of investigation: perception, visual forces, and 3D abstraction. Each faculty member has a wide range of discretion in defining these zones of study. We only begin our exploration of these areas after we have completed the establishment of the creative learning community. This includes the students introduction to the following concepts.

Creative Thinking: 12 Concepts

There is a great deal written on non-linear and creative thinking: many publications describe both its importance and processes. Lateral thinking and multiple possibilities are at the root of our continuing investigations into creative thinking. Here are 11 concepts that are discussed and used for creative problem solving. Over the course of the semester, I lecture on and provide short workshops on these approaches to creative thinking. These concerns help the students to continue to change their habitual response to problem setting and solving. These activities and discussions provide students with tools to push their ideas beyond primary considerations, to find new vantage points, produce multiple options, and restate problems. Producing multiple solutions to a single problem and re-stating the problem are all effective means of changing habitual responses.

Creative Thinking Menu: A Short List of Possibilities

Multiple Perspectives: It is important to recognize that we see the world through our own narrow experiences, habits, and memories. Seeing is judgmental. Learning to step out of our own eyes and see the world through the eyes and considerations of others stimulates creativity. To think more creatively, we need to see the world from multiple perspectives. As soon as you consider or arrive at an answer to a creative problem stop and consider a new alternative solution, then a new answer, then another new answer. This is the right of first refusal. You refuse to stop your creative thinking process at the first second or third idea. Create multiple ideas and perspectives, and never stop at a single idea.

Reading Cultural Inscription: Much of what we learn to say and do is determined by pressure: political, social, peer, commercial, and economic. We swim in a sea of culture whose currents affect how we act. These outside forces help to make up our identity. Often, we are like the ventriloquist's dummy--manipulated to act as scripted by others. Learning to read this cultural pressure and understanding how it defines us is an important step in overcoming domination and learning to speak our own minds. What are the pressures that guide our thinking in a given situation? Do we accept these pressures? Do we want to combat or emphasize these external forces? Who benefits from the cultural pressures? We need to understand the social, economic, cultural, and political forces in play and design our responses and projects accordingly.

Brainstorming: Brainstorming is creative play. It is a process of seeing possibility and not conclusions. In conversation, we allow our thoughts to flow from subject to subject, unbounded and random. People involved in the dialogue do not usually take notes on what is being said.

Brainstorming can also be random, flowing from idea to idea, but all of these variations should be recorded. What is not of use today may be important tomorrow, and all ideas are opportunities. Problem solving differs from brainstorming in its focus and relationship to creating a proposed outcome. Problem solving is bounded by the need to solve a particular problem and answer the specific question asked. Extraneous ideas are limited to what is determined to be significant. Brainstorming is a process to arrive at multiple perceptions and opportunities but falls short of defining solutions. There is a natural flow between conversation, brainstorming, and problem solving. One process slides easily into the next and flows back again.

When evaluating brainstorming, success should not be measured by the solutions offered, but by the number of ideas, possibilities, and opportunities presented.

Collection and Research: Creative thought is stimulated by reactions to ideas, visual material, data, and information. This is why brainstorming is effective in groups. Group interaction leads to multiple perspectives and experiences being brought to bear on the problem. Research deepens thinking, yet students often rely only on their imaginations to solve visual and creative problems. An uninformed imagination will produce stereotypical answers to visual and creative questions. In socially based artistic practice, it is important that the artist goes out into the neighborhood to meet the people, as well as does academic research to inform their vision. Through collection and research, the mind is informed, and past experiences are challenged and balanced.

Non-linear Thinking: Our public-school system seems dedicated to teaching to the test. They divide education into individual subjects and teach information and related skills in categorical structures. Retention of information and logic are privileged over discussion, creativity, and possibility. Creativity and non-restrictive discourse are repressed by reliance on a step-by-step progression.

Non-linear thinking is thought that is differentiated by simultaneous growth in multiple directions. An oak tree grows from a single acorn, which produces a structure with roots sending nutrients up the trunk to the leaves, in an organic hierarchical system. Non-linear thinking is more animated in its process. Like a rhizome such as bamboo that can pop-up and grow independently. In lateral thinking the thoughts jump from one topic to another each connected yet independent and self directed. This thought process is more focused on the big picture than on the details. Non-linear thinking can throw out the stated problem and reinvent the project so that it may have little relation to the original assignment.

In design and social practice, non-linear thinking is a core process, which is balanced by logic. Logic moves the investigation from brainstorming to problem and solution, which moves again to create an action plan and finally secures a conclusion. An almost complete absence of non-linear thinking practice in the American educational system leaves students with a creative thinking deficit.

The growth of bamboo is hard to control. People who know this are careful to warn others of the annoying ability of the plant to show up in seemingly impossible places. Bamboo is a perfect example of a botanical rhizome, a plant with a large root system that can create sprouts at any point. Many times, these outbreaks of bamboo occur far from what appears to be the point of origin.

French psychoanalyst Felix Guattari and philosopher Gilles Deleuze developed a postmodern philosophy that explores the idea of non-hierarchical growth between random points of knowledge, based on the reproductive patterns of a botanical rhizome. As expressed in the second volume of their *Capitalism and Schizophrenia* series, *A Thousand Plateaus*, Deleuze and Guattari say: "Any point of a rhizome can be connected to anything other, and must be." (1)

Guattari and Deleuze explain their ideas through an interest in de-regulation and de-construction of energy flows, as well as matter, ideas, and actions. Creative thought functions like the rhizome philosophy of growth. Artists take advantage of connections between seemingly random points, where unexpected ideas can easily occur. A de-centered network of energy can encourage artistic growth as well as organically occurring growth. (2)

In general, practicing the ability to form abstract mental connections and use non-linear thinking to envision or imagine the project is essential. This supports the development of multiple avenues of approach in considering an arts action. It is the process for listening and brainstorming with others and drawing out several very different ideas and reactions for a project. After ideas are acknowledged, one can discuss them all simultaneously. This process shows respect for all contributions, and it acts as a method for arriving at the theme and structure for the final project. What may start out as a mural project with elementary school children might end as a video, in the form of a performance, projected on the exterior of the school. The video serves the same purpose that a mural would, but the media and presentation are different.

Chance Operation: Composer and artist John Cage was an early prophet of many forms of art and creativity. He said: "consider chance as an attempt to achieve something natural. Consider chance operations as a means of making a decision and how relinquishing control changes the outcome … Chance, by helping to avoid habitual modes of thinking, could in fact produce something fresher and more vital than that which the composer might have invented alone." (3)

The artist may see their world with different values, cosmic comedy, and insight where others may see only the objective reality. The artist often works to overcome negative mainstream social points of view, in the forms of devaluation and disregard to self and others. Chance operations integrate frequently within this mode of thinking and designing. They take away the value system of judgment for the artist and the non-artist and replace it with an unexpected intersection of opportunity a cross-roads of possibility.

In the early 1970s, at the Maryland Institute College of Art, Hugh Merrill had the opportunity to work with John Cage and speak with him about the creative process. Cage put a great deal of emphasis on allowing chance operations into the work itself, and also into the thinking that occurred during the process. He clearly saw that overly engineered thinking led to predetermined outcomes, which were often shallow and unexciting. By leaving the creative process open to new opportunities provided by chance, the unexpected collisions of ideas and experiences relating to the original concept could be greatly enriched. He saw that it was not always possible to think or work your way to a creative outcome, but instead, acknowledged how the creation of multiple experiences brought about unexpected results which would open opportunities for further exploration and insight.

Reversal: It is easy to describe how an object could be made, but how would someone not make something? How can ideas be reversed in order to come up with a new way of approaching a problem? How would I make a self–portrait? Compared to how would I not make a self-portrait? The land of not is bigger than the land of is!

Reading the history of an object and deductive reasoning: Sherlock Holmes used his powers of deductive reasoning to solve fictional crimes. He filled the gaps between clues by reading their hidden story. Deduction is the ability to look at objects and know their history. Deduction is informed imagination. It allows imagination to move beyond labeling, to understanding past functions and origin. Deduction is also a method of critical evaluation in considering the quality of design, function, and aesthetic value of an object.

Collaboration: Most of our work in art school, is evaluated on individual achievement, authorship, and a uniqueness of vision. Much professional creative work is collaborative. The disciplines of design, film, animation, music, and socially relevant art are collaborative intersections between groups: clients, artists, designers, technicians, and communities.

Simply throwing a group together to do a project will not necessarily lead to good collaborative practice. Collaboration has to be taught. In order to collaborate, you must learn to be open and share. Learn to listen, and stimulate the imagination and voice of the people contributing with you. Too often, collaboration is taken for granted, but it is a complex social interaction marked by ego and a narrow understanding of outcomes. Much of what our society and culture have taught us in western society is that the lone individual voice is the one to be highly regarded. Learning to turn off these deeply embedded systems of thought are difficult, to say the least. The student should progress through a series of experiences that counter learned habits of individualized thought and production. Collaboration is based on service to others.

The land of Not and the land of Is: A correct and habitual answer is what can be thought of as the land of is: it is a stereotypical right answer. "What is a soccer ball?" We all know the answer to the question. A soccer ball is a specific object. Everything else that is not a soccer ball lives in the land of not, simply because it is not a soccer ball. Interestingly, when children want to play soccer and there is no soccer ball available, that does not stop them. Almost anything can become the ball: an empty can, a ball of rags, a tennis ball, or an empty bleach container. The creative answer most often is in the land of not, instead of the land of is. Asking students what they would not do to solve a problem can serve to open the field of discarded possibilities.

Language: Language can be a barrier to creativity. To name something categorizes its function and place in the world. Language is a concept for a real thing or action and not the thing itself. We may know what a ball is and be able to recognize and describe it in scientific terms. To really know what a ball is, you have to kick it, catch it, throw it and so on. A kiss is even a better example. To be able to name something is not the same as knowing it.

To see something in a new way, the automatic acceptance of a literary description or definition is not enough. Learning to rephrase and restate questions or descriptions, while considering new ways of defining and thinking about the action or object, is what makes it meaningful.

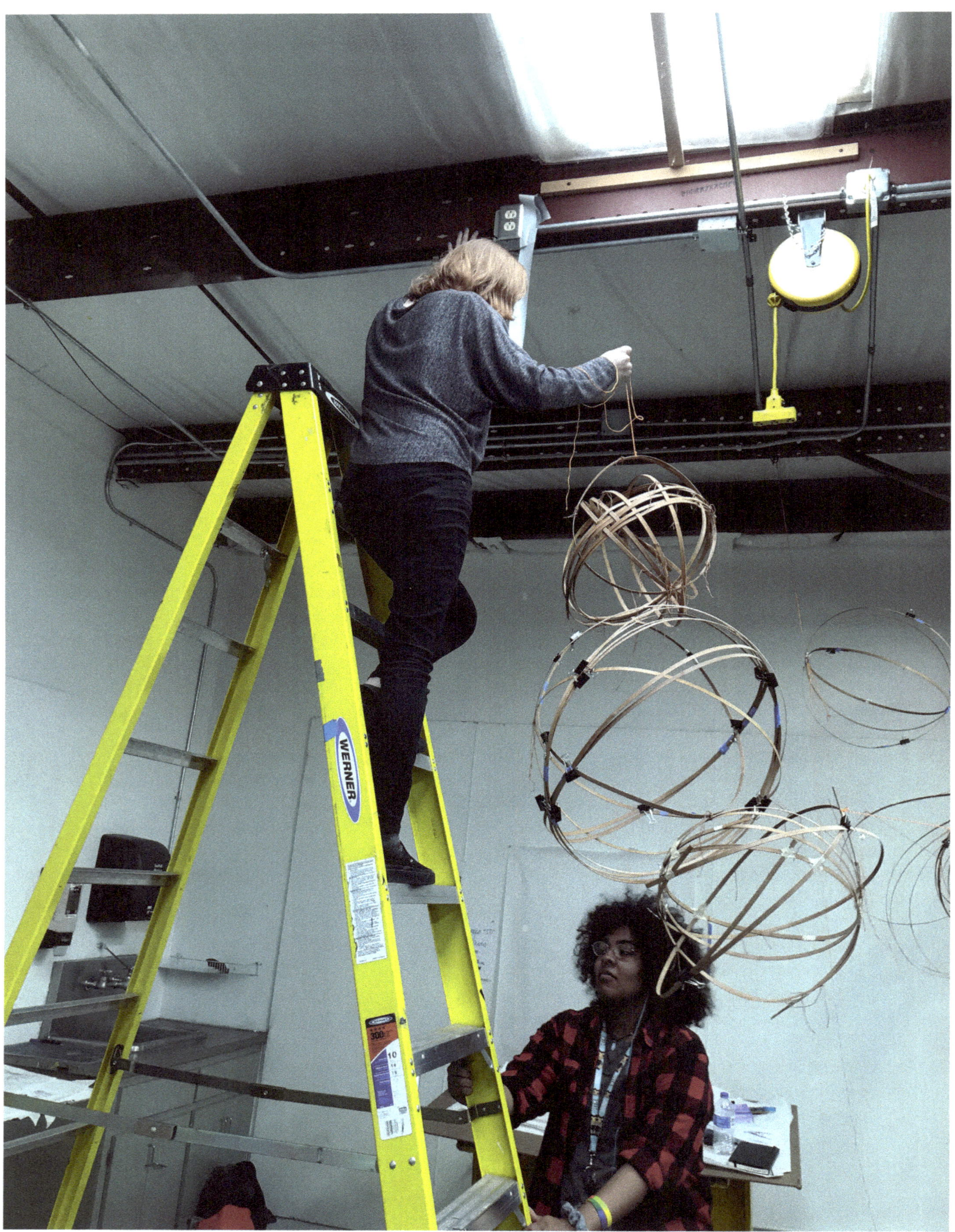

Studio rings projects

CONSIDERING HARD WORK, CRAFT, and LATERAL THINKING
IN DEVELOPING FUTURE ASSIGNMENTS

Developing future assignments requires a consideration of not only content and skill but on modes of thinking and creativity and connected cultural research. I use the following "guide" to developing the thought process behind the studio assignment.

Labor is shoveling gravel into a bag. It is arduous and takes a degree of resilience to complete a day's grueling work. Some assignments are based on this form of rigor, and demand one fight through the work to accomplish the task. Great craft is often built on this meditative repetitive working pattern. I refer to this as turtle brained work, as it is steady and continuous. It often helps win the race.

Its opposite is **rabbit brained,** darting about the field finding multiple possibilities, shooting from left to right, with short bursts of action and short periods of rest. It is thinking that is fast and spirals back and forth in all directions. Quick thinking, without critical judgment, is essential to creative development and studio exploration. It is the compliment to turtle thinking, with its consistency and focus. Rabbit thinking is grounded in possibility, not production.

Spontaneous thinking: Are children spontaneous? Perhaps but perhaps they are more chaotic than spontaneous. One way to think of spontaneous activity is to think of repetition. A great basketball player, dancer, painter, or ceramist does not have to think of the next move they know it through the repetition of body knowledge. They have done the action over and over be it physical or conceptual. Without forethought they know the action that needs to be taken. This is not physical alone for repetition of creative work leads to a deep intuitive conceptual and spiritual knowledge of the process, far beyond problem solving. It is a deep knowing and that is spontaneity.

Research: Aesthetic and Historical is looking to past works and artist to understand their reaction to a process and or problem. It includes looking at possibilities for gestural drawing, Bauhaus graphic design, perceptual or photo-realistic drawing. The process demands the replication of the aesthetic form so as to better understand its visual properties. Further conceptual research puts the work in context focused on time, place, use, possibilities and its place in culture. Such study and experiences teach the student that all forms exist in time, have a reality in the present moment and enrich us as artists. Little is self-invented and most is appropriated, re-contextualized, or re-purposed for the present reality. Our creativity and self-expression are connected to society/history in multiple facets.

Craft and Skill: covers a great deal of territory. Teaching basic skills like Photoshop, how to use the band saw, how to throw on a wheel or how to cut a wood block have set procedures that must be raised to the level of craft. Acquiring the skill to do the process is the first step to attaining a greater intuitive knowledge that leads to aesthetic quality. It is the ability of the student to move from the mechanical to a highly intuitive process. At this level, the hand and the eye have attained body knowledge. The hand and the eye understand intuitively when a piece of wood is sanded correctly. The eye and hand of the craftsperson is very well educated. Perception of a material is based on this knowledge.

Some of my assignments ask the student to render large realist standing self-portraits wearing plaid clothes and standing in a fore-shortened position. This is a turtle-brained, highly crafted assignment and takes focused repetition and labor. Other activities, like make a drawing like the crack of a whip using water on pavement and then photographing it, are rabbit brained actions. All of my assignments will have aspects of turtle, rabbit, craft, and skill. They will also emphasize connecting the process to the broader cultural and society through research and flow easily between digital/ photographic and physical material processes.

Core Curriculum and Assignments

Once the students have established a community, they feel comfortable in discussion and safe in presenting themselves and their thoughts.   After they develop basic skills in thinking and challenging their primary patterns with lateral thinking processes, we move on to the core curriculum of the KCAI Foundation Department.

The department is divided into three basic areas of research: perception, visual forces and 3D Abstraction (sculptural forms). The content of these broad areas of concern are defined by each faculty member and less so by the department. The content and assignments are part of an ongoing faculty discourse and we work closely together to vet our ideas and teaching approaches.

The ideas I have laid out-- combining of skills, lateral thinking, research, conceptual and social content--will be demonstrated in the core assignments I provide the students. We begin with perception. The preceding text is partially taken from the perception Zine I provide the students. The text allows the students to seriously consider the meaning and expanse the term perception encompasses. This text and the ideas described help the students to all have the same core conceptual information from which to consider both the assignments and the territory of perception as a concept.

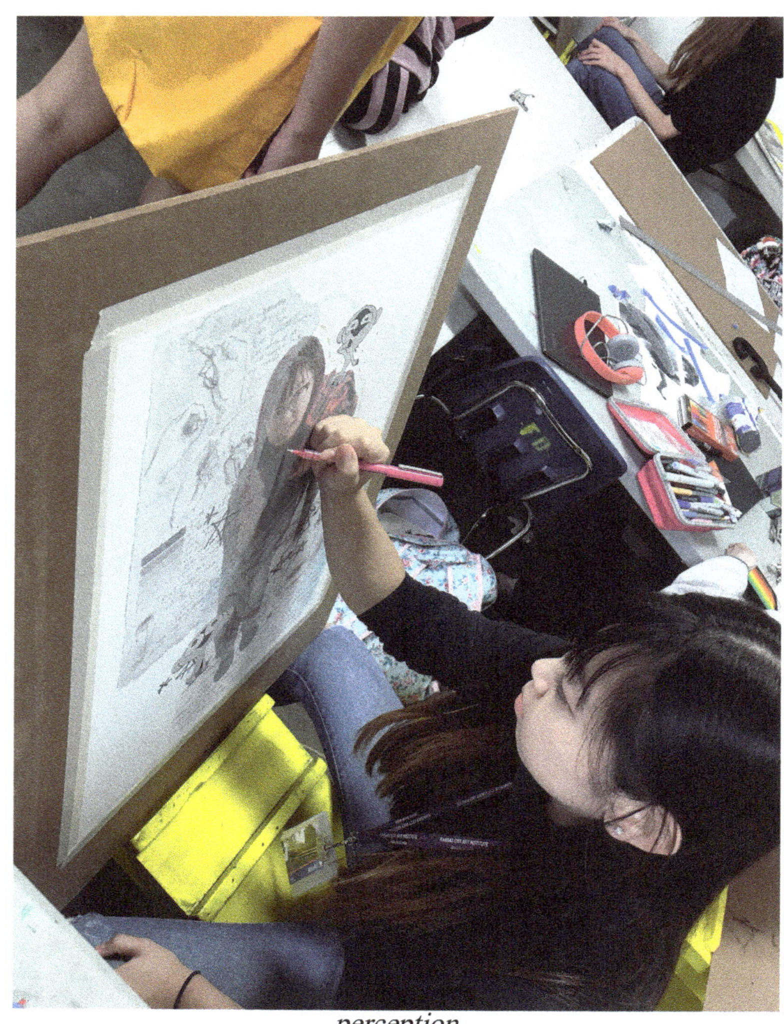

perception

3 Perception: Concepts of Seeing

Per`cep´tion

1. The act of perceiving; cognizance by the senses or intellect; apprehension by the bodily organs, or by the mind, of what is presented to them; discernment; apprehension; cognition.

2. The faculty of perceiving; the faculty, or peculiar part, of our constitution by which she has knowledge through the medium or instrumentality of the bodily organs; the act of apprehending material objects or qualities through the senses; - distinguished from conception.

3. The quality, state, or capability, of being affected by something external; sensation; sensibility.

The definition of perception includes all of our senses but for now we are primarily interested in visual perception. I suggest that visual perception goes beyond the optics of the eye to include the cognitive and conceptual function of unearthing immediate understandings and judgments on the value of what we see. Therefore, seeing is by its nature an intellectual act. I do not see a twenty-dollar bill in the gutter as trash.

Perception/seeing: Seeing and making are fundamental to artistic and creative intelligence. It takes no skill to see the world uniquely, each person is by their nature an individual and there for experiences and sees the world uniquely. It takes knowledge to see the world creatively and skill to produce a series of "marks" to communicate your creative vision.

Perception will focus on creative seeing/thinking, capturing/drawing, variation/sequence and developing a visual vocabulary to articulate and understand visual communication. Our studio work will include assignments in Photorealism, drawing from the model, abstract drawing, Photoshop digital collage, and other possibilities.

Perception in a Consumer Society

In *Seeing Power*, Nato Thompson states,

> *Everyday the culture industry- movie studios advertising firms, social media conglomerates and so on plucks the fruit of art and activism's labors and ingests it, and regurgitates a new substance for the voracious and growing nest of consumers around the world. What we like, what we do, what we listen to, what we dream about, the world we hope for —even the terms by which we define ourselves and the world around us- is increasingly controlled by huge complex economic forces.*

We live and create in a world where all forms of individualism become flattened into mass cultural production, sold back to us as a way to establish *self-identity*. The pressing urge for individuation collapses into the maxim: *we are what we buy*. The problem is broader than the ideas of artists and thinkers being co-opted by media and having these ideas commoditized by the cultural industry. Cultural production is based on advertising creating the desire and styles for *self-identity*, then generating the sounds, forms, and products to support that identity. Thompson explains,

> *The intensification of advertising and the rise of TV, radio, film, video games, affective labor, music, software and other content delivery mediums have slowly yet radically altered the entire spectrum through which we understand and perform our daily lives.*

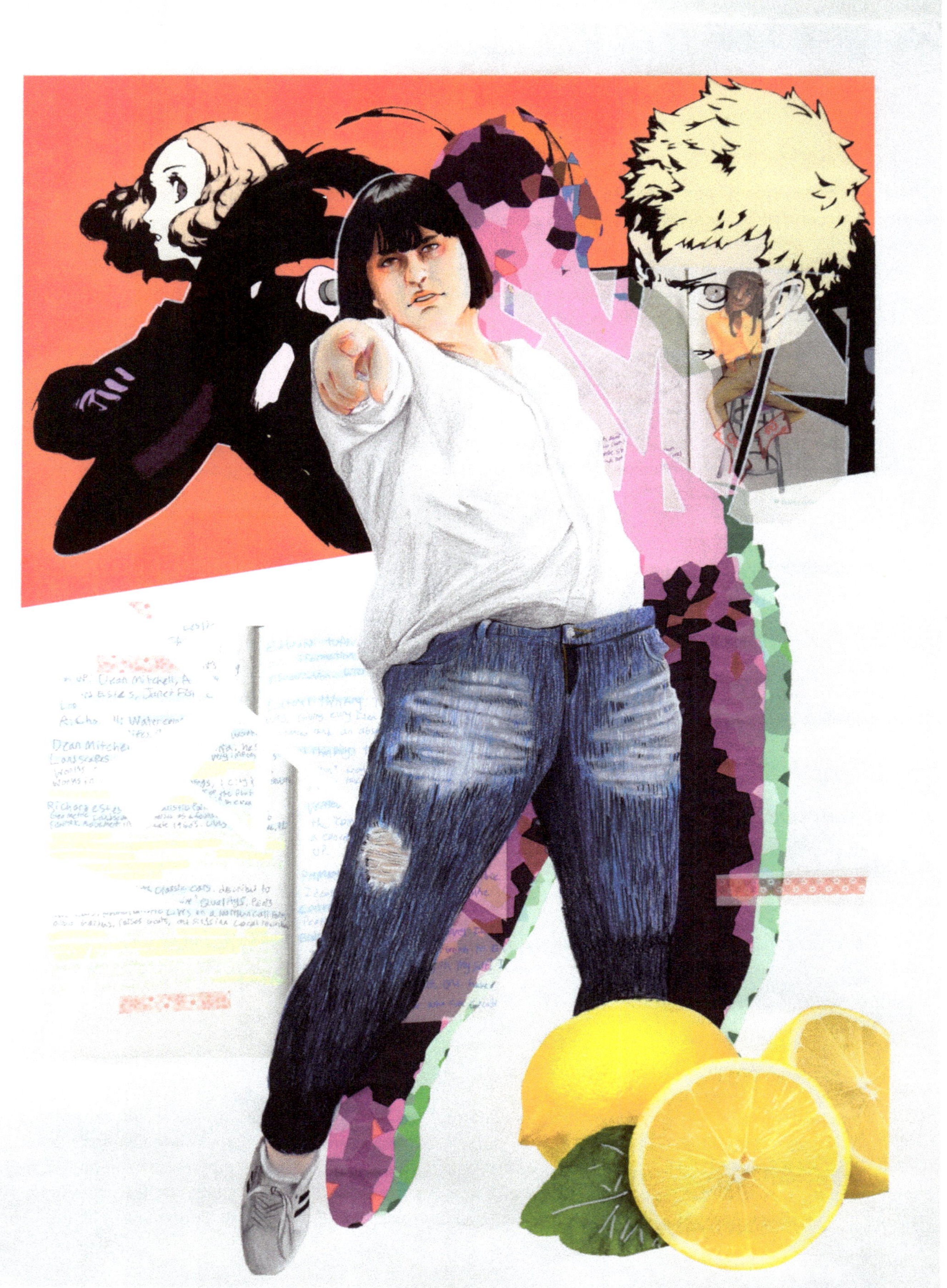

Jessica Cook

We are not only defined by what we do but by our participation in cultural capitalism. To perceive the self and the world clearly, we must understand that power arises from control over cultural production. Fox news, pop and media culture, Google and Facebook as well as Urban Outfitters, drive our realities. It is not who we think we are but which demographic identity we have been assigned by marketers that describes us. In this pre-described world, primary thinking thrives. Primary thinking is accepting what we are given and how we are defined by others. It is also what we already know and we stay in primary thought patterns by accepting the realm of our knowledge complete as is.

A secondary level of thinking requires questioning and seeing the relationship between the individual and the culturally produced commoditized consumer. Questioning our definition of self, art, creativity, news, what is good/bad moves us toward a higher level of inquirers. Seeing what is the sub-text behind the consumer culture is a secondary level of thought challenging the obvious and easily understandable.

Further, we are defined by other institutions and cultural lenses: church, region, ethnic and racial background, economic class, rural or urban backgrounds, and family experiences. We are also defined by the genetic gifts from past generations, including our body type, hair color, disposition, gender, selection of sexual identity and more. All of these go into making us who we are and it is this awareness that moves us to a second level of perception and thinking. Secondary thinking is recognition of the complexity of perception. It is questioning the given definitions of our society. To question is the precursor to the third level. The one we will reach this semester.

Third level thinking stems from actively seeking and utilizing a broader investigation of the world through research, interaction, making, failing, variation, and doing it over again. The third level is to make, to think and re-make and consider the complexity of meaning again. It is not stopping at what you want to do but moving far beyond that point of departure. It is not accepting the first or even the second version of an experience or idea. It is not working merely to complete the assignment and get a grade. It is working to learn and form new patterns of investigation. The third level is learning to make, learning to research content, and making again. It is openness to chance and exploration through committed studio work. You must commit to searching out what you do not know, researching the unknown, constant daily journaling and questioning and being open to possibility and new experience.

There are perhaps many ways to consider how we see from optical to conceptual. Here are nine conceptual possibilities for understanding how we see/judge/perceive/think. You can add to this list your own conceptions on modes of perception.

Ways of Seeing Conceptually

Seeing through memory: We see what we are programmed to see by our past experiences. In short we see what we are looking for, seeing is about need, desire and is erotic by nature. We see through attraction, some element that we need or desire controls our gaze.

Seeing through language: What we see we can name. The names are only symbols for the objects, moods, places, experiences we see. Language is not the thing, object or experience we see but a representation of experience. Naming helps us value our experiences, organize our thoughts and memory. Seeing through language is symbolic, pragmatic and intellectual.

Seeing through intellect: seeing is an intellectual act, it is never neutral, seeing is an act of judging and assessing value, of determining, categorizing and thinking.

Seeing through image: is a primary step in seeing creatively, here we see visual relations and forms that step outside of language and memory. Visual literacy is seeing the abstraction of the "picture" in our view. Our view can then be considered and we see in sequences and patterns, we can see the world before us as composed of visual elements not just names. We are learning to see relationships; we see form and color, diagonals, straight lines, masses and motions.

Seeing through materials: we see the image before us, perhaps a landscape, not just as light and color but imagined as a set of marks. We can learn to see the image through the materials we hold in our hand, pencil, paint, ink, photo, charcoal, or watercolor. Processes be it photo, digital, film or video and others are also materials and alter the way we think of an image.

Seeing through aesthetics: we have knowledge of the aesthetic of the materials we are using to create the image. We see by envisioning the images as a quality of aesthetic memory, we can accept or reject the envisioned aesthetic quality but that quality is inherent in our vision. We are seeing and understanding what we see through the knowledge of the marks and images of past art and artists. We have a standard of values which influences of vision.

Seeing through imagination: imagination is informed by perceptual and conceptual seeing and envisioning, Imagination is seeing the "real" as skewed, altering the expected and the known. Placing the known in a new and unexpected light.

Seeing through compassion: is the ability to see through the eyes of the other, the defeated and disadvantaged, and not to just see a disadvantaged person. It is to see the causes and circumstances that lead to a person or group being disadvantaged. It is not simply serving soup in a soup kitchen to the homeless. Benevolence/kindness while a good thing often gains more for the one who gives the soup than the one who receives the soup. Seeing the cause of the situation and solving it is true compassion.

Vision: is the combination of the above governed by intellect and intuition based on the hard work recording/processing your experiences, then communicating those thoughts and images to others.

Perception can be divided into areas, here are 3 examples:

Optical: We see objects and spaces when light hits our retina producing a fuzzy, flat, upside down image. This unreadable image is turned to electrical energy, moved by our nerves to the visual cortex and then other places in the brain to be instantly processed. Turned into a clean and meaningful image that we take for granted.

Psychology of Perception: refers to interpretation of what we take in through our senses. The way we perceive our environment is what makes us different from other animals and different from each other. We will discuss the various theories on how our sensations are organized and interpreted, and therefore, how we make sense of what we see, hear, taste, touch, and smell. For now let's be aware seeing is an intellectual act, involving judgement, memory and experience, it is not merely optical.

Gestalt Principles of Grouping: The word "Gestalt" translates to "whole" or "form," In order to interpret what we receive through our senses, we attempt to organize this information into groups. This allows us to interpret the information without unneeded repetition. The Gestalt principles includes four groups: *similarity, proximity, continuity, and closure.* When we look at 6 red dots and 4 blue dots on a white background we see two sets of dots not 10 individual dots. Gestalt is visual organization and understanding patterns.

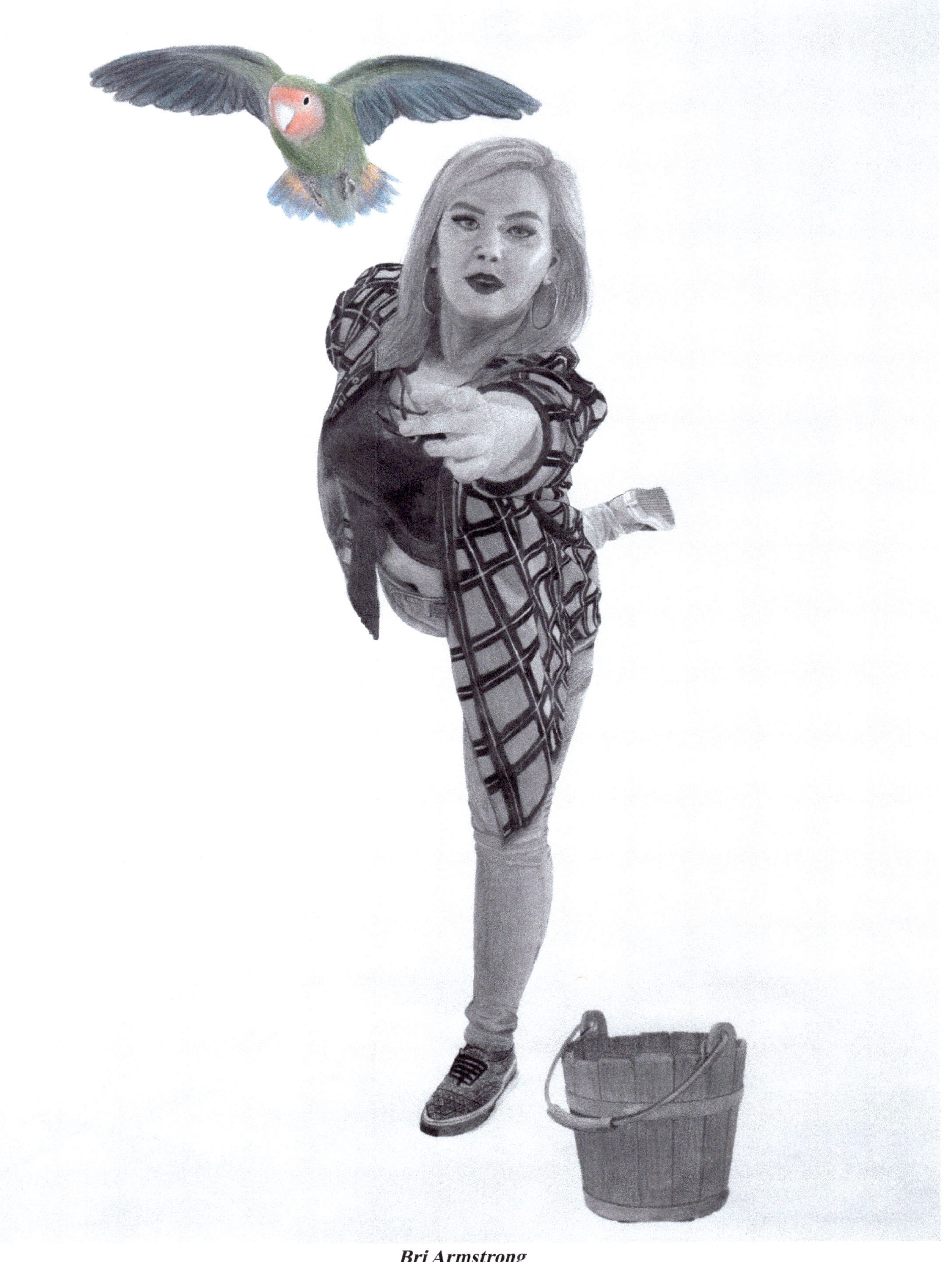

Bri Armstrong

Realism and use of Photography/Photoshop

In the paintings of Caravaggio, 1595 and a century later Vermeer the optics of a projected image were traced onto the canvas creating photo realistic paintings. These paintings while realistic also are mystical because the eye understands space, proportion and other visual relations much differently than the single projection from mirrors and lens. Western Art has always been connected to science, optics, realism and verisimilitude. In teaching the student to use cameras to capture images, use Photoshop to explore and develop the image for printing or projection onto paper or canvas the student is learning important lessons in perception. On how the eye works and what the camera captures that the eye cannot easily register. Realist image making considers how the eye works differently from the single lens of a camera.

Considering Realism: Photography and Photoshop

We use drawing, photography and Photoshop as a means to understand perception and not only as a goal in itself. We think about the way the eye and mind work in unison to create meaning, concept and representation. About half of the class will have a significant knowledge of Photoshop and the other half know a little to nothing about the program. The same is true with drawing skills there is a group that has spent significant time drawing from life or from photographs and a group that has little drawing experience. The realist assignment calls on students to use and learn both Photoshop and drawing at the same time. This again unifies the community by allowing most students to work from their strength for at least part of the assignments.

The assignment begins with the students being photographed standing in a foreshortened position with hand or leg extended towards the camera. We introduce the student to the very basics of using a 35mm DSLR camera. The photos are shot in the KCAI Foundation Department shooting studio with basic overhead lighting. The photos are downloaded from the camera to Google Drive and the students are asked to go in and download their photos to their computer or storage device.

For many this is their first introduction to a shooting studio and use of a professional camera that shoots raw files. They are provided a packet of information on converting and shooting Raw files. At this point we do not focus on the technical concerns of using the camera, and understanding file types. These concerns will be covered in detail as we move through the semester.

The students are asked to take the files and open and save one as a Photoshop file. For many this may be their first introduction and use of Photoshop, for others they are well versed in the program. Our goal is not teaching Photoshop directly but using Photoshop as a tool. The students who do not know the program are taught how to use it for this specific assignment. This process provides them the opportunity to successfully use the program in a limited range yet lays the groundwork of basic understanding and opens the door for further learning and exploration.

We do a learning assignment that teaches a series of important Photoshop, printing, and Google search skills that will be needed for the self-portraits. The students are asked to do a Google search for an image of the American Civil War. Take one of their self-portrait photos and place themselves seamlessly into the photo. They must select a photo that is 4MP, 2272x1704 that equals to a 10x8 inch image at 300dpi. Here we go over the importance of image size and what size is usable for digital collage and for printing and what is a useless thumbnail. We go over how to do a Google search for images and visual content. They must take their full color self-portrait photos and turn them into grayscale files, here we introduce the basics of using levels and curves to edit and improve or change the photo. They are asked to cut their image out from the background and save is as a separate file. They then move their image into the civil war photo and using free transform to resize themselves to fit seamlessly into the image.

Again there will be students who know how to use Photoshop for digital collage and graphic design and others who know it for the dark room opportunities and those that have no experience at all. The goal is to provide the confidence and knowledge for extended self-learning and understanding how to research visual information for digital collages.

The assignment can be done in one class session with the more advanced students helping the less informed students. I have them repeat the exercise and make sure that each student successfully understands the learning outcomes.

For homework they are asked to repeat the exercise and use a color file and put themselves on stage with a rock or rap star. Next, they are instructed on how to print the works as 11x15 laser prints on archival paper in the KCAI print center. They purchase a sheet of Stonehenge paper from the school store to print out their two images. During class the next day they take the printed images and are instructed to take sand paper and sand down the images, draw back into them with pencils, charcoal, color pencils and paint on them with acrylic paint. We discuss the works and the creative process of combining photos and drawing. Most important is making sure that all the students have achieved the goals of understanding how we used Photoshop, printing, Google search, file sizes, and working back into a digital print. All of these skills are required for the upcoming large standing self-portraits.

Assignment 1: Self Portrait

The students are then asked to take one of the raw files and convert it to a Photoshop file. Remove or cut out the back ground leaving only the figure. Save the file as a 12x18 inch grayscale file and adjust the tones to achieve the greatest degree of tonality from rich black to a pure white in levels. Print as a resource for doing your larger 18x24 inch pencil drawing. Then they resize the file to be printed on a 18x24 sheet of drawing paper. They reduce the opacity of the file by 70%. Print the file on the drawing paper and render in the richness of the tones to make a photo-realistic drawing with pencils.

The students are asked to:
- Auto correct the color file and save it
- Cutout their figure using the polygon tool
- Make a 12x18 laser print in grayscale mode
- Save the cutout figure to a new document 18x24 as a grayscale file.
- Adjust the opacity to 30% or lower and print
- Print the 18x24 image with the figure standing in full view approximately 16 inches tall
- Print the jpg at full opacity as a 12x18 laser print to use as a resource from which to do the drawing.
- Do separate laser prints of faces hands and other important areas as a resource for the drawing
- Complete the drawing rendering in all the tonalities with 6H-8B pencils

Learning Outcomes

The picture plane is now understood not as a flat 2-demintional surface but is seen as a spatial box moving both forward and receding in space. The figure standing at an angle pointing the hand in extreme foreshortening toward the viewer is not a mere series of shapes and patterns but is the representation of a 3d form defining the blank background space surrounding the figure.

It is important for the student to understand and experience the range of gradations/tonalities moving from white to black in 8 to 12 steps. To see and understand these tones in both the drawing and in the photograph. Tonality in the photographs are adjusted with level in Photoshop to achieve a range of tonalities.

Simply drawing a step grid of tonality from white to black is a good exercise and is turtle in nature it is as much about labor as learning to see gradation of tones. Here we use the Photoshop eyedropper to grab all the tonal variations in their photo image. We then arrange them in boxes from white to black. This makes them look deeply at a work of art, their photograph and see how varied the tonal range is.

The rendering of the image takes persistence and time and the student must use the pencils for their range of individual tonalities. They come to understanding the importance of building up tones with repeated strokes of the pencil. They learn how to gradate the tones from light to dark in the rendering of fabrics, hair and facial features. They learn to make the tones flow seamlessly from white to black through the process of rendering. The rendering accomplishes a number of exercises related to tonality, pressure, and the darkness of a mark.

The use of the printed photograph evens the field for all the students, those with drawing knowledge will produce very realistic works those that have come to the college with little interest in drawing and or experience are able to achieve a very realistic image. For all the students the success of the assignment builds confidence that they can use what they have learned with success. It produces a community that is not overly competitive in a negative way. Further it demonstrates to all the student that they can draw anything no matter how complex, If it can be photographed, reworked in Photoshop it can then be traced and drawn and is accessible to their image making.

Assignment 2:

The art historical and contemporary use of photo-realistic image making is covered by my lecture on photorealism referring to the book *Secret Knowledge* by David Hockney. This lecture demonstrates the long history of artist using mirrors and lens to trace images to achieve photo realistic images. The students are asked to research the work of *Chuck Close, Dean Mitchell, Richard Estes, Oscar Ukonu and Juan Francisco Casas Ruiz.*

The full assignment is as follows: We discuss how the eye has difficulty seeing complex patterns such as plaid shirts and especially if the patterns are wrapped around the human form, We refer to David Hockney's *Secret Knowledge* and the paintings of chainmail on figures in old paintings where the artist uses lens to capture the correctness of these complex steel linked patterns. In the next stage of the assignment the students are again asked to photograph themselves but consider how they are dressed. They are asked to wear clothes that consider color, tone and value changes, have wild patterns that would be difficult to draw perceptually, to again stand in a foreshortened position, to place a coffee cup or small object in front of their foot. The relation between the cup near the student's feet and the pose reinforces spacial depth in the picture plane. They sometimes wear a hat or carry a staff or hold another object in their hand. They are asked to cut the photo of themselves out from the background and adjust it in levels as a grayscale and as a color file. They are asked to find an animal that represents them or simply one they find interesting. To use Google Search to find a high-resolution digital image of the animal and cut it out and in Photoshop, collage it into the image of themselves with the coffee cup. They follow the same procedure as in the prior assignment reducing the opacity and printing the image on archival drawing paper then rendering the image with a set of pencils from 8B to 6H.

Assignment 3: photorealist digital collage

Many of my assignments are repeated but made more complex and allow for the student to have greater input into the outcome. The student is never given an assignment to simply do what they want. There is always a solid framework to preform within and boundaries to push against. The assignments also asked the students to stretch their conceptual ability and search for an answer. Many assignments take them to the edge of their understanding. They want to have clear directions so they know what the outcome or final project will look like. They in reality need throughout the semester to struggle with arriving at a concept. I point out that they need to find several possible solutions, then we discuss their choices. They need to move beyond being "worker bees" and do the heavy lifting of developing a multi-layered, self-driven assignment. Yet the assignment must fit into the learning outcomes and scope of investigation we are working with. It is never simply doing what they want based on their past successes. Their conceptual work must require research, lateral thinking, multiple options, and not a single solution or work produced on their first inclination. They need to learn to be self-starters and deeper thinkers, this is very hard work.

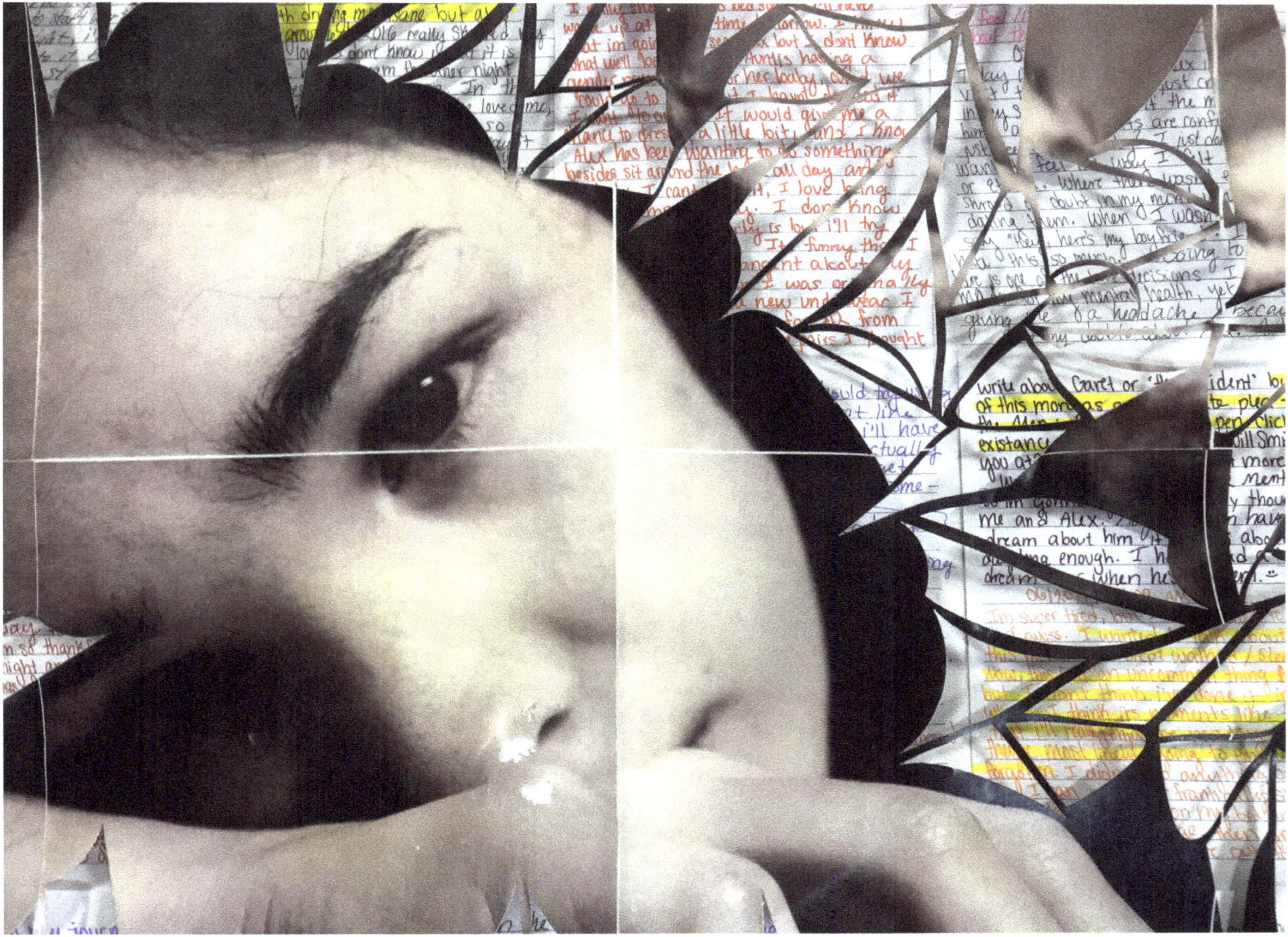

A Portrait of Self

In the third iteration of the realist drawing assignment they are asked to do *a portrait of self* from their standing poses, add text, personal information and cultural information. They again cutout a color image of themselves in a standing pose that is printed as a transparent image to be drawn back into with color pencils. They then add scanned in pages from their journals and sketchbooks and use a Google search to find and add text and cultural imagery. The final image is a digital print on archival paper 22x30 inches that they can work back into as needed. The assignment covers all the processes, and many of the exercises they have recently experienced as well as hints at processes of graphic design (visual forces).

They all easily understand what a self-portrait is but a portrait of self, containing the above information does not provide a ready-made primary answer for the students to work from. They have to struggle with the concept and come up with various solutions. I do not easily clarify the assignment but allow the class to discuss possibilities. I ask them to write down three ideas for how they might approach making a portrait of self. We then read these in class and begin as a community to determine a range of possibilities. For the most part they understand narrative as a connected series of images in a single time and space. Like a graphic novel. This assignment provides content through layering rather than a literal narrative visual structure.

The final image is a combination drawing and digital collage printed on archival paper 22x30 inches. The students do the work in Photoshop reducing the figures opacity so that the color pencil drawing can be done so as not to easily reveal its photographic under image. The other content is left at full opacity. All the students experience using photography, digital collage and drawing as a unified creative process. This process of combined possibilities opens up new doors for image making for the students. When their images are printed they draw back into the work as needed using drawing to connect and emphasize the layered digital narrative. We review the work and discuss how to continue the drawing by adding a greater range of marks to emphasize areas of content.

For the most part I do not allow the students to use pop culture in their work because it is so well understood and accessible to them. It is part of their primary thinking and knowledge base, and the content is so easily understood. Here in this assignment they can use pop cultural images because the pop images are disturbed by the realist drawing, layers of content added from their journals, family photos and or sketchbooks. The pop reference is not the center of the narrative but only a component changed by its association with personal journaling and the realist portrait.

We look at Alfred Leslie, Kiki Smith, Robert Rauschenberg, Larry Rivers and Kerry James Marshall and discuss their use of line, imagery and text. Based on what they have gained from the review and the discussion they continue to complete the drawings. The final critique is not descriptive as most of our discussion have been up to this time but is based on overall quality, formal relations and content. Here they learn to read the possible content in the images and describe what the layers of marks and imagery might suggest. They are in a good position to take on the critical task of analysis of the works do to the progression of first learning a descriptive professional language, then adding content to their own works by layering visual information and not simply creating a concrete linear narrative in time and space. For the first time they can call on their memory and feelings about the works. This coupled with their growing understanding of formal and descriptive visual language leads to a successful critique of the works in the studio.

By this point all the students have achieved a fundamental grasp of Photoshop including how to save and save as, documents, how to change from RBG to Grayscale how to change contrasts with levels and how to find high resolution images on the internet and use them in their collages. They have also made a habit of searching on Google and looking at multiple works of the artist they have been introduced too. As well as selecting images for their resource image files. They have begun to make the connection between the assignments and the use of the processes and ideas discovered in visual research/contemporary art. This work provides an aesthetic Foundation for their critical thinking as well as a connection between our experiences in studio, contemporary cultural and art history. They have begun a studio practice that flows easily between digital collage, printing, drawing and mark making. One is not prioritized over the other. They have learned to layer content using cultural images, journal writing, and photo realist drawing. Those who need to build their Photoshop skills are directed to our self-study online workshops and with their beginning Photoshop experiences and confidence they are successful in learning new uses and skills of the software program. The strength of the community that has been developed is also very important at this stage with those with more experience in Photoshop helping those with less knowledge. All the students have reached a high degree of self-confidence because of the success of their three realist drawings and ability to work successfully in Photoshop.

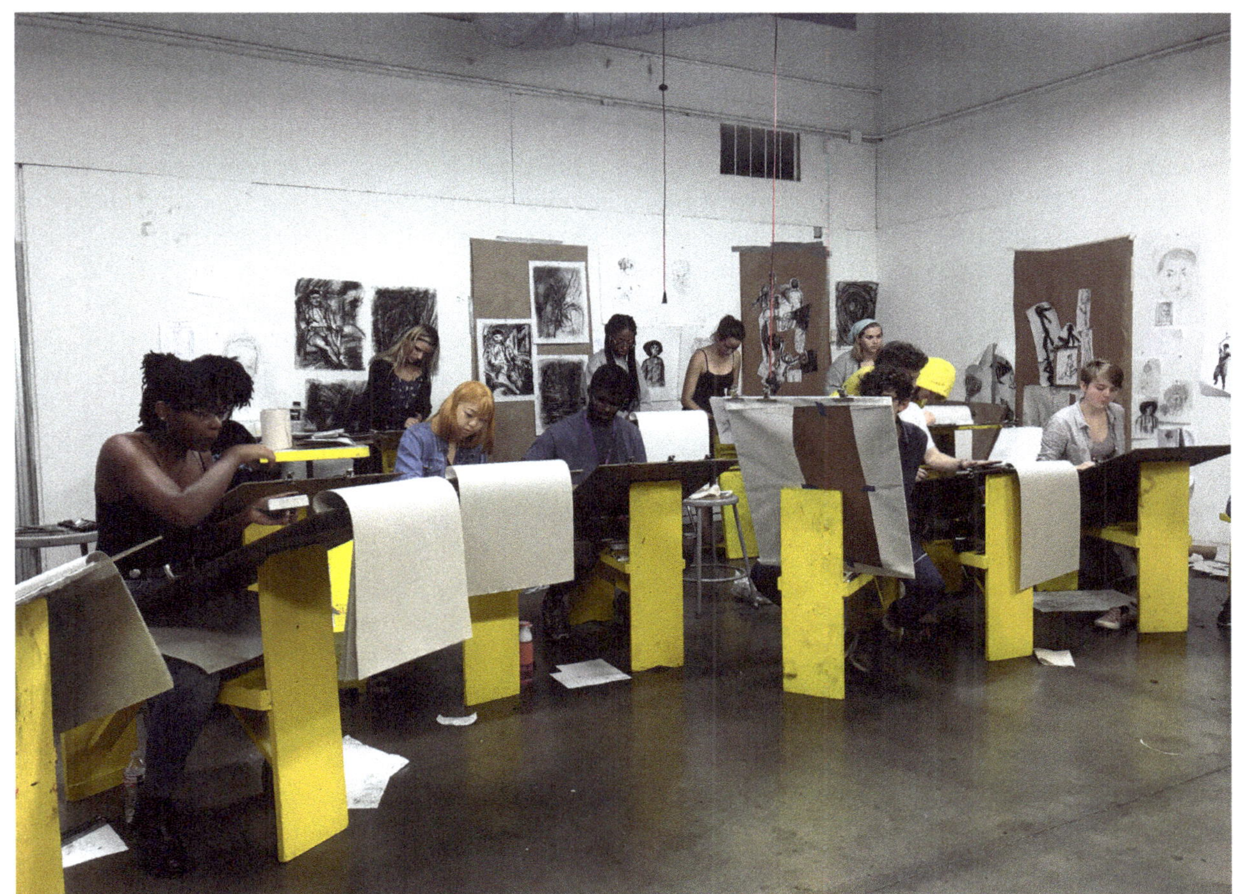

Drawing from Life

The class by this time now knows how to work with concentration in studio and has begun to grasp the meaning of professional terms to describe and critique visual images. We at this juncture make a shift to drawing from the nude model using ebony pencils, charcoal and erasers as mark making tools. This part of the course uses the figure but is not merely a figure drawing workshop. Drawing from the nude is a method to teach gesture, contour, blind contour, proportion, abstraction and use dark to light lines to create form. We continue to focus discussion around perception examining how we see. It is almost impossible to look at the model and draw at the same time. There is an instance of memory between looking and focusing on the paper to make a mark. Perceptual drawing is related to the movement of the eyes between the viewing of the model and the mark making on the paper. It is a negotiation, a repeated searching out the correct forms in the drawing as related to the pose of the model.

The students for the most part, are in the habit of drawing with the muscle memory they use for writing, in short they draw only from their hand and wrist creating lines or contours that outline the figure as a shape. This is their comfort zone. We discuss this reality and talk about drawing from the elbow and shoulder with force and movement. We attempt to create lines that have life and emotion and are not simply contours.

Assignment: Normal Line +

I ask them to draw three lines, a normal line, one that has the delicacy of an eggshell, and one that has the explosive power of a bomb. Most if not all the students draw three lines that are very close to the mark they would make if writing a letter, Many try to draw the shape of an egg or the shape of an explosion like a mushroom cloud, I point out that these are symbols for egg and bomb but have no emotional expression in and of themselves, that all of their lines are of the same value, width and length, Mostly the lines are 2 to 3 inches long and are straight. I ask them if this is the visual range of their emotions? They laugh.

Then I use a sheet of paper pinned to the wall and an ebony pencil. I draw a normal line it is unlike there's, the line is long continuous, is thick and thin, curves back on itself and does not stop. Then I do a line as light as the ebony pencil allows again it is long continuous and curves. It is in no way the shape of an egg. There is slight thick and thinness to this delicate line. Lastly, I smash the pencil into the paper and move my arm with great pressure and speed not picking up the marking tool so that the violent mark I make is explosive, jagged, rich and black, aggressive and violent. I say now that is a range of expression and again in surprise they laugh getting the point.

Most understood the correct answer prior to my demonstration but they are not in the beginning willing to express themselves so they stay on the safe side of the problem by drawing a simple "normal" line. This exercise will come in handy when we begin to draw gestural and contour drawings from the model later in the day.

Gesture

At this point the model is asked to do a series of gestural poses each lasting for 10 seconds and the student is to capture the gesture of the models pose. They find this very difficult on the first day and most return to outlines or contour drawing of the figure. I have to go from drawing bench to drawing bench demonstrating to each student the difference between gesture and linear contour. Show them how to draw from their elbow and shoulder. How to make a gestural mark that responses to the gestural pose of the model. If the students are sitting at the drawing horses, I ask them to flip the horses up and draw standing up to force them to work more from the shoulder. It takes time but they begin to get it and to understand the word gesture as a physical reality and not a vague concept. This assignment will be repeated at the beginning of each drawing session for the rest of the two-week session.

Blind Contour: Learning to Look

The model is asked to take a series of 3 to 5 minute poses and the class does blind contours trying to focus on where their eyes are "seeing/touching" the model. This is a looking exercise and again the students have a great deal of difficulty in not looking down to adjust their charcoal and or ebony pencils. Over the 9 classes in which we use the model they will experience these methods of seeing and mark making. In the beginning we stress gesture, contour, blind contour, and using the hard plastic eraser to introduce subtractive mark-making.

The home/studio work is based in abstract mark making based on the work in class with the model.

Assignments:

- Using charcoal respond to a drawing of natural forces by Julia Merhetu. They are given several different copies of her black and white drawings in pen and ink, the students have to respond to the work using charcoal and erasers.
- Fill a page with thick to thin lines drawn from the shoulder,
- Draw the power of being inside a tornado without any representational forms, no cows floating by on the wind
- Use charcoal to produce a black sheet of paper then erase it back to gray/white
- Take three of your gestural figure drawing and use them as a resource to create an abstract drawing, (we have in class and in the museum looked at the Abstract Expressionist works as an aesthetic model)

Each morning we review the evenings work but do not critique it. At this stage of looking it is not important if it reminds you of something and it is not important that it is evaluated as good or bad. We simply describe the drawings using professional terms from the glossary. I give out a cheat sheet of words that best describe the drawing activity of their abstract and figure drawings. Here they are able to understood in language the words and their conceptual meanings that we are using to describe the drawings. The class quickly and clearly understands the drawings that work better than others simply by using the descriptive language. Students begin their comments with the phrase "what I like about this drawing is" At this point this is ok over the semester we will move away from this safety phrase for beginning their description. I want them to comment and talk with as little fear as possible.

Each day we return to working from the model and stress gesture, contour, adding and subtracting marks, quality of lines and marks. We end the daily workshop with a longer pose and allow them to approach it as they choose to. The vast majority try to draw the figure realistically, in proportion and with detail. I allow them to draw from the model doing 20 minute poses at this stage of investigation. Here they can work on seeing, proportion, shading, and striving for a realistic/perceptual interpretations of the poses. At times we add deep shadow through altering the lighting and using spot lights to cast dark shadows. Yet the next day we always return to gesture and more abstract mark making.

I provide copies of various artist such as Alice Neale, Bernard Chaet, Larry Rivers, Alfred Leslie, Grace Hartigan, Elaine de Kooning and others for them to copy for their evening studio work. This again connects them to art history in an experiential way and provides content for aesthetic understanding for the exercises in studio. We continue moving from copies to perceptual drawing adding more complex visual settings, and continue daily the quicker abstract drawings using gesture and blind contour. The repetition is very important to deepen learning.

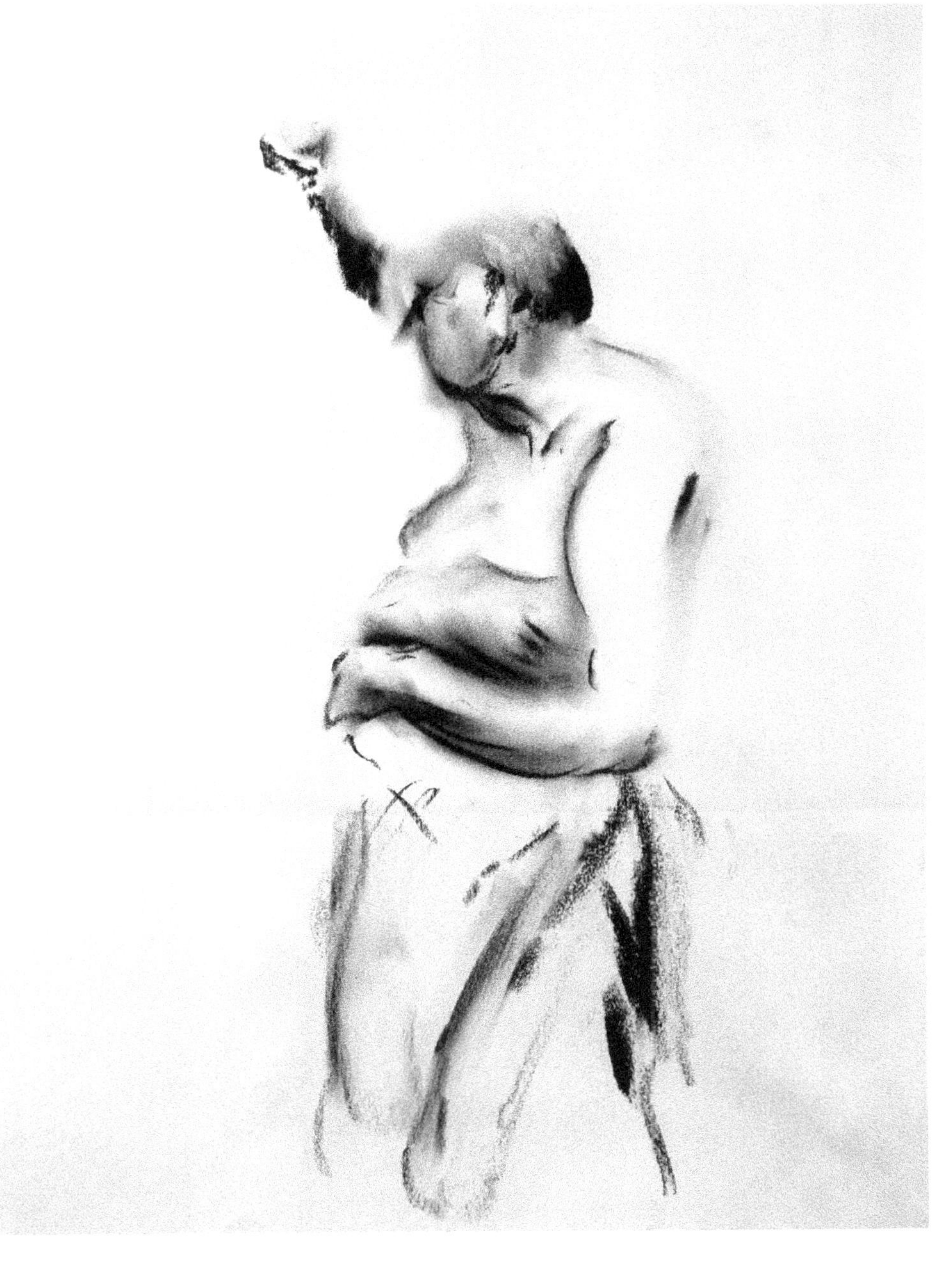

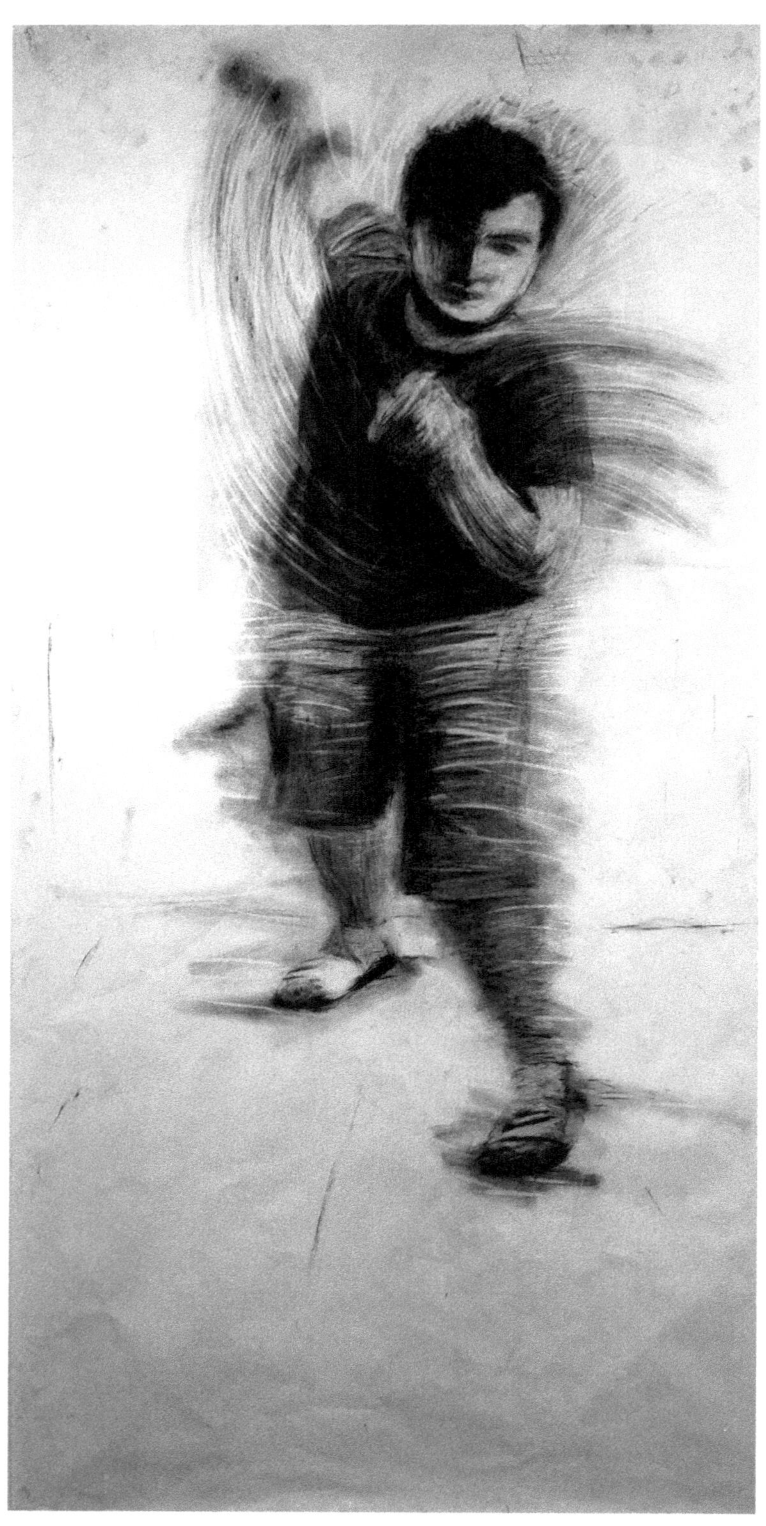

student drawing response

Projection, Movement and Blur Ending Exercises on Perception

As we move toward the end of the modeling sessions, I re-introduce processes we used in the photo-realistic assignments. They are asked to take a photograph of themselves in a dancing, jumping, swinging and moving pose. There is a marked difference in drawing the model in motion or doing gestural drawings that have the feel of motion than drawing motion.

Motion is one of the factors that the camera can pick up that the eye cannot record with specificity. The photos are done so as to capture the students jumping, falling, dancing, swaying, twisting with specificity. These images are not blurred. We take the photos that accurately describe the body moving from being stopped by the speed of the camera and we put them in Photoshop as grayscale files. We then use the motion blur tool in filters to blur the photographs selectively. These images are then projected onto large sheets of white roll paper provided by the department and the student's outline as best they can the soft blurred edges of their projections. They print out 11x17 blurred images as a resource and work to complete their large charcoal drawings.

Here we extend their experience with the use of charcoal and erasers to make abstract passages that replicate the feeling of blurred motion. We have used the project to reinforce the use of photography, Photoshop, self-portraits, mark making; abstraction, tonality, and basic drawing skills. We discuss the differences in modes of perception such as when to use the camera and when to use only the eye and hand.

At this point in the semester everyone has developed a basis for understanding terms in the glossary, has developed important Photoshop and Camera/photo skills, has experience in drawing, is use to making remaking, creating variations, lateral thinking and the ability to describe artworks and visual images in formal terms.

Discussion in and about perception will continue throughout the remainder of the semester including conceptual, optical, technical and cultural aspects. I cannot emphasis enough that the three areas of investigation Perception, Visual Forces, and 3D abstraction have important overlapping content.

4 *Visual Forces*

Foundation

WORKBOOK

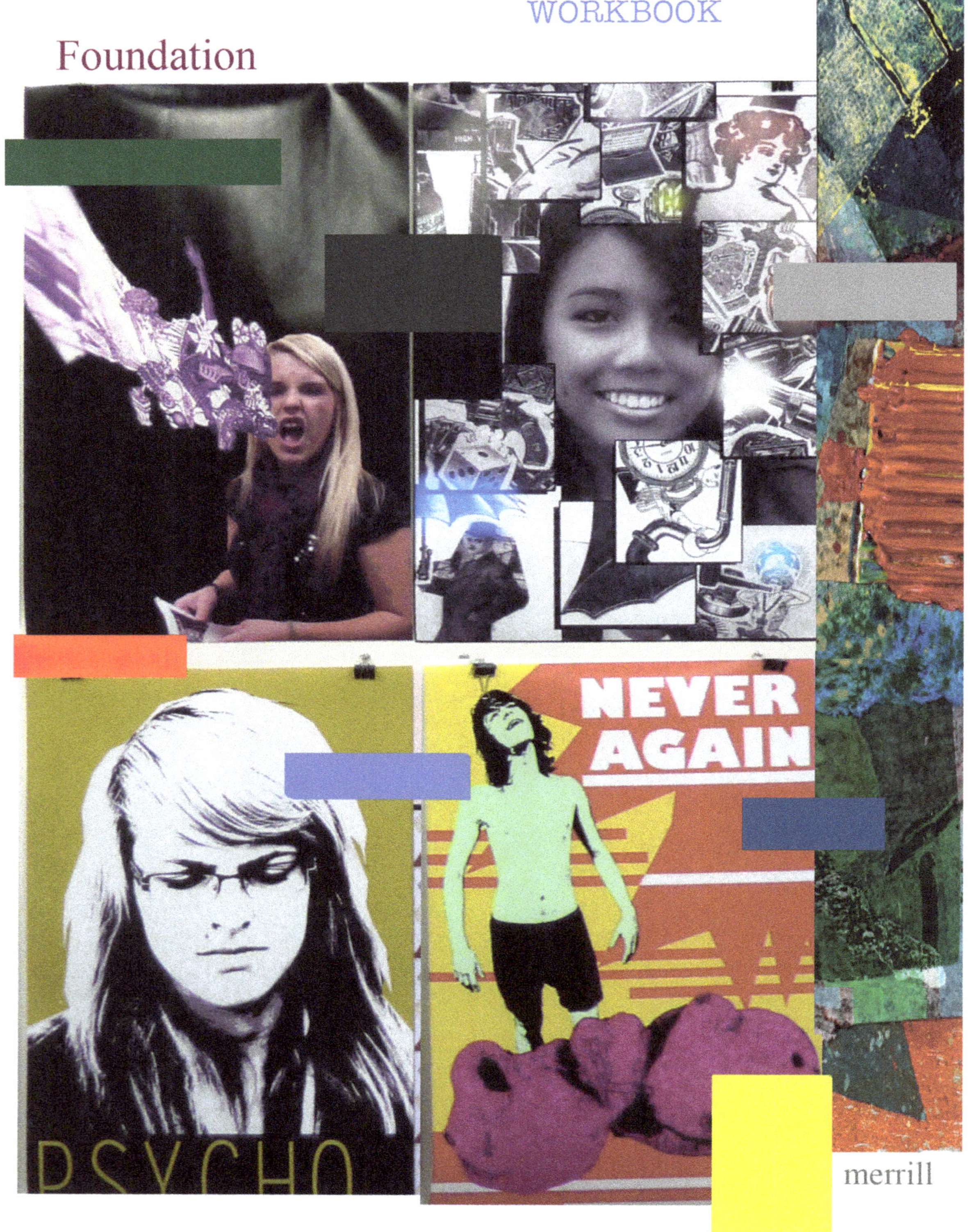

merrill

Visual Forces is an introduction to design concepts, communication and information graphics as a visual language. Visual Forces is a broad term for design activities and tools. Design is complex and covers advertisement and social practice solutions to human and community problems. Those activities and tools have changed in major ways since I went to art school. Graphic design was taught then as composition, the relations between letter forms, positive and negative space and other "graphic concerns". Design is a major conceptual area that evaluates society, art, consumerism and capitalism. It is not simple composition or even graphic communication. Today design in all of its formats defines itself differently and as a form of social practice. Designers are artist helping people, communities and other clients to communicate, collaborate in finding solutions and determining the scope of problems. Design is also the appropriation of images that through juxtaposition lead to new meaning or re-contextualizations of images and idea. The graphic images of the late capitalist system reach out to hail the consumer, make them look at products that are meant to reinforce their desired lifestyle and fulfill their desired sensations.

Much of this content has been touched on in the Perception section of the Foundation curriculum and will be continued in the final 3D Abstraction section as well. The concepts and exercises are interwoven into many lectures, workshops and assignments. A process that deepens and reinforces learning. The overall curriculum and each section Perception, Visual Forces and 3D Abstraction are designed to engage students with a wide range of experience and interests. The core assignments in this section will underscore the relationships between cultural concepts, communication, and graphic design principals. Social practice concerns are brought into the learning curve through an assignment working with an external community. Over the past year we have been working with the Veterans Writing Team of Kansas City. Details of this assignment will follow below.

Visual literacy is concerned with visual communication, the language of design, the use of materials and digital collage and printing processes. We will look into the history of design and graphic communication as an aesthetic resource for the assignments and solutions. The course is primarily taught from the western cultural point of view. We live and create in a diverse and multicultural society and will reference other important cultural approaches and reference as a part of the presentations and assignments.

Basic Design and Visual Literacy Language

Much of the following basic information is provided to the students in the form of a printed Zine so that they are provided with the basic conceptual definitions for design. It cannot be taken for granted that all students will have been exposed to these terms and concepts and the list of definitions and simple explanations assures all students are on or near the same page.

Form, Shape and Space

When we look at an image our built-in cultural instinct is to ask what does this series of shapes and forms ***mean.*** This habit stops us from seeing as visually literate artists and designers. We remain in a realm of primary thinking and seeing. We miss important layers of significance and possibility. Perception, Visual Forces and 3D Abstraction are designed to transform primary seeing to a deeper level, developing the artist's trained eye. An eye that goes far beyond the first impression. This understanding is the first step towards visual literacy. Below is an outline of basic definitions for important aspects of design. These definitions are all important to our creative thinking, understanding and analysis of visual communication. Understanding these concepts is essential to designing, making and analysis in the coming assignments.

Shapes and forms are areas which identify configurations or the appearance of 2D shapes and the illusions of 3D forms in the picture plane. Two-dimensional form has width and height. The appearance of three-dimensional form has width, height and the illusion of depth.

Form and shape are either organic or geometric. Organic shapes are irregular in outline, and asymmetrical. Organic forms are naturally occurring in nature such as sand dunes or the meandering flow of a stream. Organic forms are often created or sculpted by erosion, wind or water.

Geometric forms include squares, rectangles, circles, cubes, spheres, and cones. These forms are most often constructed or human-made. They are used as building blocks to construct larger more complex sculptural and architectural structures. They are the base forms of our built environment, our cities and homes. They become more organic in nature by erosion, entropy and time.

Of course many human-made forms are also organic. Think about Architect Frank Gehry's Guggenheim Museum in Bilbao Spain. The opposite is also true, not all natural occurring forms are irregular or organic; snowflakes, soap bubbles and crystal structures are geometric and mathematical formulations. Look up images of animal camouflage, butterflies, ice and snow, sand, water and auroras.

Realism and Abstraction

When we look at an image (picture) if we recognize objects and places, we think of it as being **realistic**. If the image is difficult or impossible to identify in terms of the *realistic inclination* it is then **abstract**. Sometimes the abstract images come from a "real object" other times it has no relation to a thing or object. We often use the term non-objective in this case.

Our understanding of a realistic or known form can be altered significantly by the conditions that influence the form. Background, pattern, color relations, lighting, are a few of the changes that will contribute to the understanding of the form. Visual emphasis affects our sense of what the image means. Changes in visual qualities can change the meaning and content of a form.

Building Blocks

2D shape, pattern, form and color are the building blocks for composition including: *line, value, hue, tone, texture, figure ground, gesture, proportion, shade, and tint*. These will be explored through assignments in perceptual drawing, photo assisted drawing, creating image text works for printing, collages, silhouettes, pattern and the study of color. **The building blocks of visual images are always abstract, that is why we study them as abstract relationships. Nothing against representation! And one is not in competition with the other. They are inter-related.**

Line:, either explicit (draw) or implied (the space between two planes), it provides the contour of forms. Line can be short, long, fast, slow, gestural or mechanical, it can be thick and thin, light tone or dark, forceful or delicate, in color or gray. Made of a single stroke or multiple strokes. When does a line become a plane?

Value: is the lightness or darkness of a color. Gradated value is what we call shading that produces form or 3D illusion on a picture plane. Strong contrasts in value may define the boundaries of forms, like a black form meeting the white background space.

Hue: Gradation or variation of a color. Hue is the term for the **pure** spectrum colors commonly referred to by the «color names» - **red**, **orange**, **yellow**, **blue**, **green violet**.

Texture, is the quality of the surface, its roughness to smoothness. Texture can also define a shape on a two-dimensional surface. We can see the shape of the textured area creating its own area in the picture plane.

It is a combination of these forces that ***play*** together to determine the organization of the composition.

Pattern, Composition, Form, Positive and Negative Space

Forms and shapes can be thought of as **positive or negative**, as a figure-ground relation. The positive form sits in front of the background, a drawing of a tree and the white paper = background, implies the sky. The background is negative space. Negative space is of equal importance in a composition to form. We will work in all three area of the Fall semester in Perception, Visual Forces and 3D Abstraction with this concept of positive and negative relations.

These definitions and concepts can be dived into two areas, Elements and Principals.

The **elements** are components that can be isolated and defined in any visual design or work of art. They are the formal structure of the work.

> point
> line
> form
> movement
> color
> pattern
> texture

The **Principles** are concepts used to organize or arrange the structural elements. They are also part of the formal structure and meaning of a visual communication.

The principles are:
> balance
> proportion
> rhythm
> emphasis
> unit

> These basic design and graphic terms must be understood in relation to Post Modern design principals. Process of making and seeing rooted in appropriation and Hybridity.

Post Modern Design Principals

- **Appropriation** Using historical and mass media images
- **Juxtaposition** change meaning by contrasting images
- **Recontextualization** Positioning images in relation to pictures, symbols or text to change their given meaning
- **Layering** overlapping a multiplicity of images
- **Interaction of text and image** interplay of language and image meaning systems
- **Hybridity** multiplicity of media
- **Hybridity 2** blending of cultural sources to investigate a subject
- **Grazing** Understanding how familiar imagery is seen and understood differently depending on who is looking at the images, age, cultural background, other
- **Representation** self-identity and finding an artistic voice within history and culture

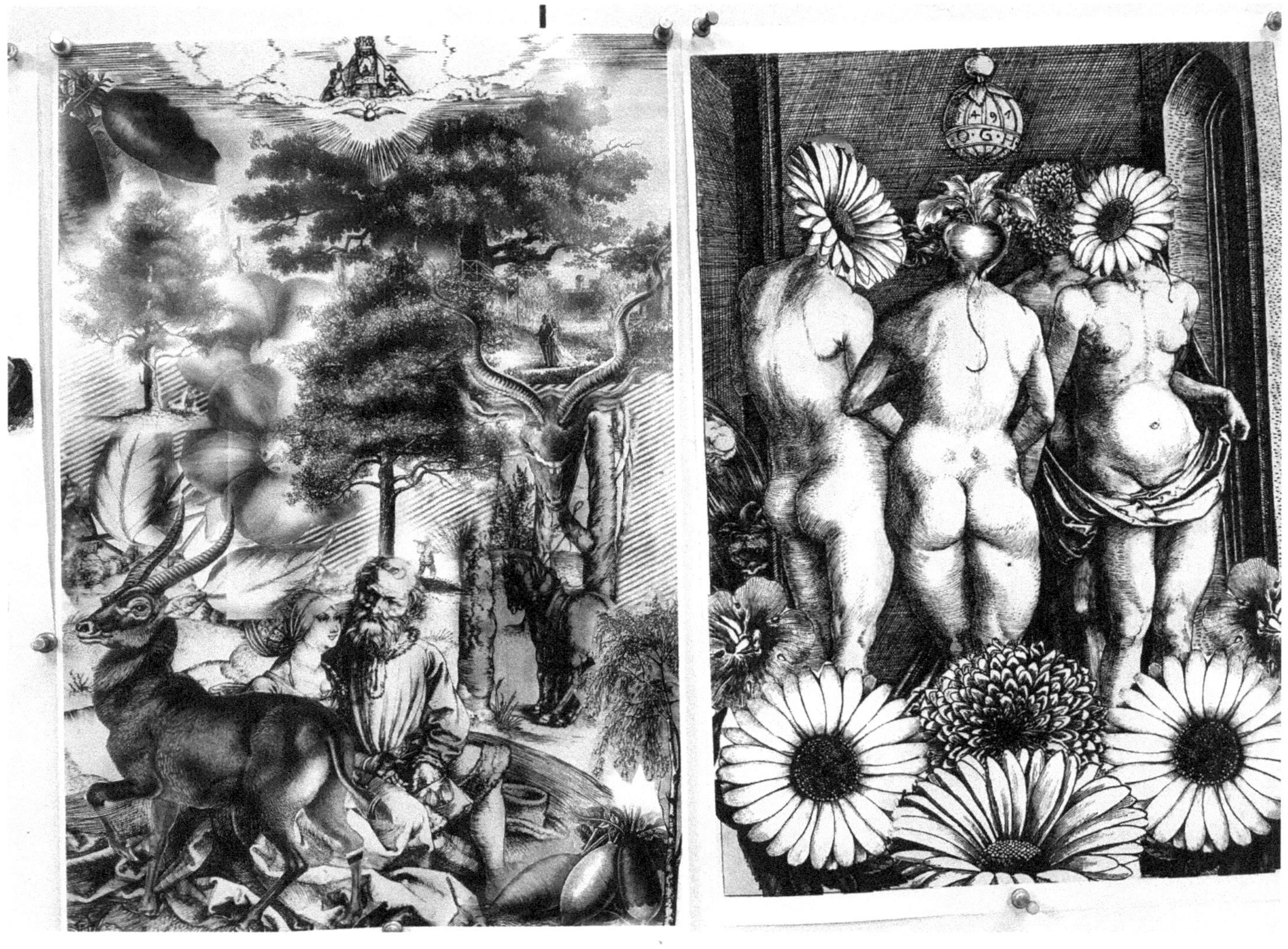

Durer response collages

Visual Forces Assignments

The above underpinnings will be the formal language we use in discussing the following assignments. In these assignments there is little selfexpression and content put into the images by the students. The educational goal is not self-expression or social political communication. It is to open design possibilities and an introduction to playing with graphic language concepts. Yet in the end all assignments lead to expression and conceptual content.

Albrecht Durer: The Language of Engraving

Using Durer's engravings as well as a combination of scientific engravings of flowers, animals, and scientific instruments from earlier centuries the students are asked to create dynamic collages. The goal is the study and experience of working with engraving's binary mark making system for the articulation of form. The marks that make up these images are either black lines or white lines/spaces. All these images are seemingly "realistic". Yet they are simply a black line or a white space. This is the language of engraving/printmaking. The marks can convincingly produce the sensation that you are looking at the fur of a rabbit, the petal of a flower, liquid in a glass container, or the anger on a face. By presenting assignments that utilize Durer's images as resources for collages the students learn the language of printmaking without the interference of skills needed to cut blocks or make etching plates. It simplifies the problem to the basic graphic language of positive and negative mark making to produce form.

The assignment also opens up the realm of re-contextualization, using existing images as the resource for making new graphic works. Finally, it introduces the student to the works of scientific illustration and of the artist A. Durer demonstrating the importance of art historical knowledge as a major factor in creative thinking. Here art history is not a series of dates and names but images and graphic possibilities.

As a continuing part of developing the student's knowledge base of referential images they are introduced to surrealist collage as a general art historical resource focusing on the collages of Max Ernst. They also look at contemporary relief prints by artist such as Tom Huck, and Bill Fick. Here the art historical, contemporary usage of the engraved mark and discussions on content including lectures on Durer's engravings connect the assignment to broader conceptual concerns. It is important that each assignment be connected to contemporary practice, art history, aesthetics and reading contemporary image content.

The students often are familiar with graphic novels and contemporary graphics found in comics. These works often utilize the binary mark making language. We investigate the works of Charles Burns, Lynd Ward's *Mad Man's drum*, and Rythm Mastr by Kerry James Marshall.

They are then asked to enlarge on a copier one of their collages or a Durer engraving, blowing up the image to capture selected complex details of engraving such as clouds, cloth, landscape or water. These abstract images, made of black and white engraved marks become the source for a series of abstract drawings with micron pens. This exercise trains both the eye and the hand to experientially understand the engraved binary graphic language.

The curriculum moves through a sequence of assignments beginning with studying binary mark using engravings as a resource for drawings, collages and digital collages. These exercises move to studies of mountains and flowers done by replicating and working from Chinese masters from *the Mustard Seed Garden Manual of Painting by* Chien Tzu Yaun Hua Chuan 1679-1700. This is a 6 to 9 hour studio project where the students are given copies of mountains, waterfalls, landscapes and trees to reproduce using brush and pen. There is strictness and repetition to drawing and working with an engraved black and white linear language. Chinese brush and ink has commonalities related to the engraved process of using multiple parallel lines to describe form. Yet it is marked by fluidity but still demands a great deal of control. The two system of representation are related in their use of black and white mark making. The learning outcome is the same as with engraving, to train both the eye and the hand to experientially understand the graphic language of brush and ink painting. Again, opening up the student's vision to new possibilities of mark and image making.

As with other assignments the drawing is complimented with digital collage and printing. The students scan in the images from Chinese landscape and mountain brush paintings and create digital collages that are printed out as 6x24 inch scrolls. Again we simultaneously use drawing with pen and ink, and brush and ink, then use scanning images for digital collages. The students are able to spend 3 to 4 class hours making variation of the Chinese brush paintings again "playing" with opportunities provided in Photoshop. The multiple variations are an end in themselves. It is creative variation, and the repetition of changing the same base image that is important. At this juncture I give a lecture on Deter Roth's printmaking and postcard variations of a base form to demonstrate the possibilities of this creative process.

This is a process that allows for deeper looking and repeated viewing of the Chinese master ink and brush drawings. All the work in Photoshop reinforces what they have learned in the drawing and painting exercises. The final assignment is first practiced in studio with the student's making the brush and ink drawings of rocks, water, flower, and mountain forms in class. Then the studio evening work is to make a final well considered 12x24 image using brush and ink turning the mountain forms into an investigation of abstract drawing. We return to the work of Julie Mehretu and Gabor Peterdi as an example of drawing from nature to create abstract forms.

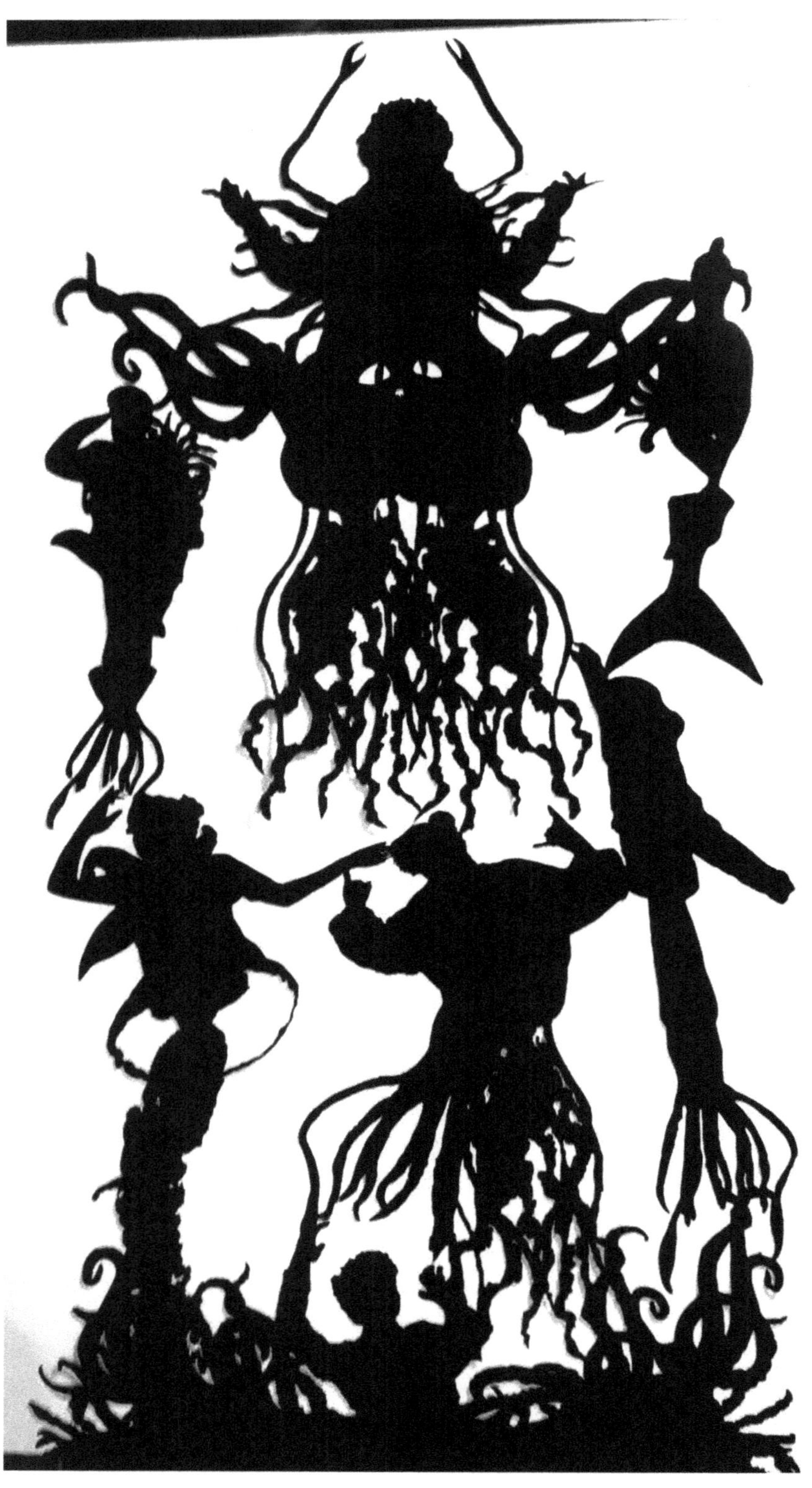

Collaborative silhouette installation

Black Line to Silhouette

From these, collage and drawing based assignments focused on engraved black line and brush and ink paintings we move to creating images from silhouettes. The focus is first on creating and understanding shapes as dynamic and fluid organic forms. The silhouettes are a form of experiencing and working with non-geometric design elements. The assignments are based in using forms that represent organic, fluid, supple, twisting and sinuous visual passages. Its secondary value is the development of complex narratives and lateral thinking.

Assignments

Using silhouettes found on line of Jellyfish and other non-vertebrates to create a collage that has the quality of liquid flowing forms in Photoshop and we print it out on 17x11 paper. Grid off and scale up the image onto large sheets of black railroad board and cut them out as silhouettes 6, feet by 4 feet or larger. After the initial critique and remaking session, the class is then divided into 5 groups of 4 students each. Each group is asked to create an installation on one of the large vacant walls in the Foundation building using all of their forms by overlapping and connecting them to make a large dynamic flowing installation. They often have to go back and remake new squid-based images to fill in spaces to complete their large installations.

The assignment is like many others and is given a second time with more latitude for individual content and development of narrative. They are asked to individually combine human silhouettes with other silhouetted content to produce a 4x8 foot installation narratives.

We look closely at the works of Lotte Reiniger, Kara Walker, Christian Boltanski, for the assignment as a means of developing narrative and content. Again, we discuss the individual works and determine which images would go together to make a larger narrative installation. We then divide into teams and make larger installed silhouette graphic works.

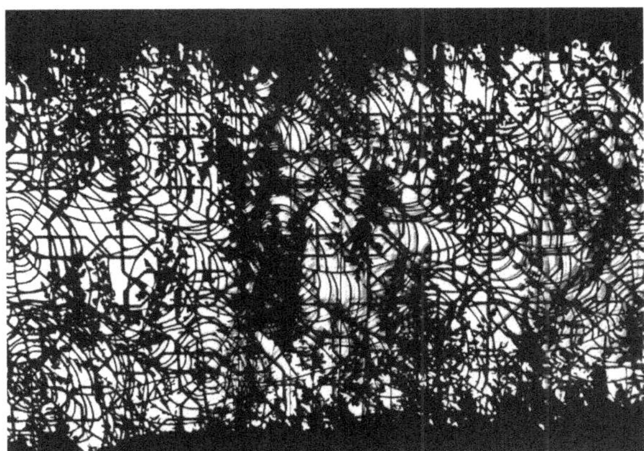

Large to Small Hand to Laser Cut

We then move from large works to small 6x9 paper cuts on black railroad board cut on the laser cutter. Each image is to have a 1/2 inch border and all forms are connected. No floating forms are allowed for this assignment. The work has to be narrative and representational and is made by combining silhouette images as a digital collage in Photoshop. Again, we look at Lotte Reiniger animations and Kara Walkers work to get a better understanding for the aesthetic needed for the assignments. The Photoshop image is then traced in Illustrator and with the help of the staff in the Beale Studios for Technology, the students learn how to produce laser cut works. When all the cut outs are produced, we do a traditional critique concerning process and content. To extend the assignment into the realm of installation we take the forms and use an old slide projector and project the shadows created by the pieces onto the studio walls. Again, the use of laser cutting, Illustrator and the possibilities of projected shadows are not pursued in depth. This is a focused, experiential introduction to these processes. Some of the students will return to this process for their final self-directed assignment at the end of the term. They will have learned enough to greatly expand on the use of digital collage cut out on a laser cutter.

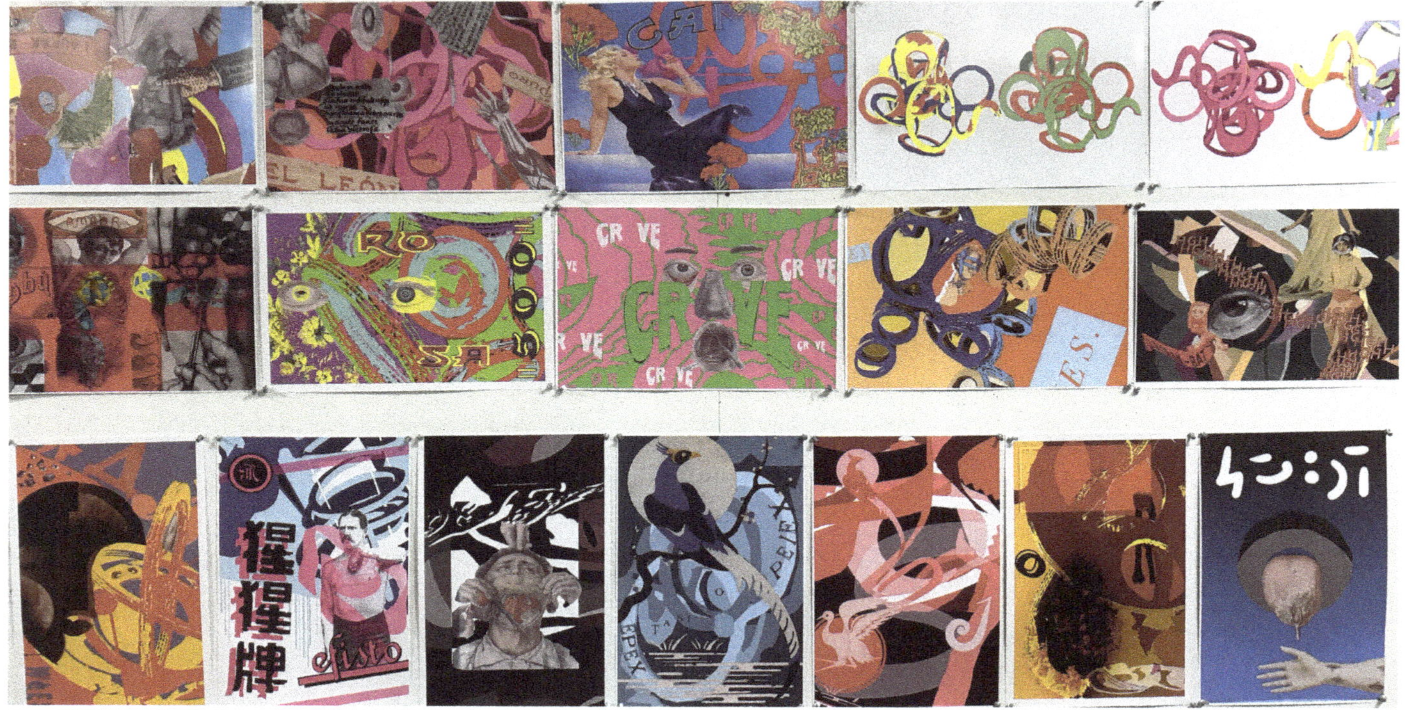

Studio Response

Investigation of Russian Constructivism: Introduction to composition, graphic design, and Post modern design principals.

These assignments investigate Russian Constructivist graphics, German Expressionist Graphics, Chinese cultural revolutionary posters and other forms of visual communication. The assignments are designed to teach a series of fundamental visual and design skills and expand the student's understanding of the international history of graphics. The assignments and experiences help the students understand design elements and principals through the experience of making and remaking graphic works. We look into the post-modern use of existing graphic forms that have been re-contextualized to produce new content and meaning. We spend time on line exploring the work of Barbara Kruger, Andy Warhal, Jenny Holtzer, Sheppard Fairey and others. These artists and historical examples free the student of believing that all images must come from their invention and that to use existing forms is "cheating". We strongly establish the post-modern process of using existing images to produce and articulate new ideas.

Here the students are also introduced to image text works and the importance of letter forms and the quality and use of fonts in design. These studio experiences make the student become sensitive to and enhance their ability to explore graphic elements and organizational concepts/forces. They achieve a higher degree to professionally analyze and more clearly discuss their conclusions about the works made both in class and by other artist/designers. This section of study sets up core visual literacy and design concepts, working processes and a language for describing and working with formal visual elements in a knowledgeable manner.

Content for daily studio exercises that supports the major assignments has included:

- Figure ground relations
- Analysis through design
- Organization of elements
- Reversal of figure ground, positive and negative form
- Shape, size, scale, proportion,
- Movement, balance and discordant forms
- Texture and value
- Pattern and intervals
- Unity, harmony and disarray
- Space in the visual field
- Letter forms
- Structured/geometric and organic/free flowing designs
- Placement and distribution
- Interrelationships of form

Other important concerns include: Detachment, touching, overlapping, interpenetration, union, subtraction, intersection, coinciding, tension and compression, visual distribution, similarity, shape gradation, union or subtraction, path of graduation (morphing), speed and direction, gravity, position of a form, frame of reference

Russian Constructivist Graphics

We begin in the digital lab with each student looking up Russian Constructivist Graphics and collecting the ones that most interest them for their resource file. I provide a talk on the use of geometric forms, photographs, design elements and the use of the tilted grid as a principal for composition. We then look up Shepard Fairey, they imminently recognize the Shepard Fairey's posters and the Obey giant symbol. I make a connection between Shepard Fairey's very contemporary works and their relation to the works done in Russia the 1900's. We discuss the meaning that lies behind this form of design and its connection to revolution. How the design by its self has meaning and communicates. The students are asked to select one of the constructivist posters to use as a source for further exploration.

Assignment 1:

Uusing red, black, white, yellow construction paper and a black and white photograph from the newspaper they make an 18x24 inch "copy" of the graphic they have selected. They explore the Cyrillic letter forms, which no one in the class can read, by carefully redrawing and cutting them out to follow the design principals of the original poster.

They write an explanation and description of the design that they read aloud to the class during the presentation of their work. This is to in sure that they experientially and conceptually understand the essence of the design process.   They are then asked to use digital collage to make a new piece based on a Russian graphics as a self-portrait. They replace the photographic elements of the original work with photographs of themselves sometimes in the same positions and wearing similar clothes and helmets as in the original work. They often change the Cyrillic text to English and invent a humorous communication. These works are printed as laser prints 12x18 inches in our print center.

Assignment 2:

The class is given two books of advertising and graphic images with which they would have little or no knowledge of. In 2018 They received *Crucial Interventions Illustrations of nineteenth-century surgery by Richard Barnett and Rolling Paper Graphics by Prageone*. As a group they collaboratively scan the images and make them available on Google Docs for easy access. The students are asked to make an 18x24 inch graphic image using images from both books based what they have learned from Russian Constructivist Graphic. The images they are using have no cultural, or deep emotive significance to the students. The images are appropriated, and content is set up through juxtaposition and recontextualization of the images. They are introduced to Barbara Kruger and other post-modern artist using design tools to hail the eye and draw attention to quick and rapid communication.

This allows the students to work with concentration on the design elements and not on graphic cultural communication. It also broadens the student's knowledge of these past design traditions and again adds new resources for graphic and image investigation. By this time in the semester the students have become accustom to researching and collecting visual resources from the past. Resources that cover both fine arts traditions and ones in the commercial and design world. They are beginning to see how the fine arts and the commercial world of advertising overlap both as re-contextualized content and as significant design possibilities. They often come to me and show me their discoveries of new visual resources on-line. This ability to expand their studio knowledge beyond primary considerations is a major step in being visually literate. Here again, we focus on producing high quality digital files for digital printing with correctly scanned images saved in the correct formats for presentation and printing.

Assignment 3:

To reinforce this I have the students look up postage stamps from prior to 1960, find high-resolution files that they can work with to create a 12x18 laser jet prints. Many of the stamps reinforce elements of both silhouettes and black line engraving languages. They are asked to use Photoshop to place themselves on a stamp. As with the previous exercise the students have to focus on downloading from the internet the correct sized digital image of the stamp they care to use. They often have to take portraits of themselves to fit the content for being on a stamp. You do not get on a stamp unless you have done something historically important, They consider this in designing and taking portraits of themselves. And again, we focus on developing a high quality file for digital printing. This project is completed in two 4 hour studio session and one evenings work and one day to have the completed image printed for the class discussion. Often they begin to express how important the digital searches are for their understanding of graphics and their future image creation.

Assignment 4: Cultural Revolution Poster

Like the Russian Constructivist poster assignment this project has similarities. The students are now well versed in the use of Photoshop and flow easily back and forth between the handmade drawn images and the use of digital collage and printing. The students are given a lecture on Chinese Cultural Revolutionary posters with workers and students holding up Mao's little red book, and Moa in the sky beaming out rays like the sun. I have over 100 such images in my personal collection and they have been digitized. The students select one image to work with and are asked to "update" the poster. This leads to a discussion on the cultural revolution and the 1960's. Next, I give a lecture on humor in art and show examples of Pop Art, use of commercial design styles in the art of the Chicago Imagist school, works printed by Raw and Zap Comics. This is to set up the content of the assignment. They are to remake the cultural revolutionary posters so that they have a high degree of humor. The USA relation to China is not democracy against communists but is all about trade. It is a commercial relationship, so many of the posters remove the red books from the hands of the Chinese workers in the cultural revolutionary posters and replace them with bottles of Coke, McDonalds burgers and other icons of America.

The first iteration of the posters are made from cut construction paper requiring the student to do exacting design work in transferring the image to the red, white, black and yellow paper to be used for the project. The cutting of separate colors has deep relations to printmaking both relief printing, silkscreen and other processes. Artist have to make a separate stencil or block for each color to be printed to complete their poster. Secondly the Chinese posters were originally wood block prints and the respect and history for printmaking runs very deep in China and these attributes are pointed out in the lectures as the students make the posters. Lastly the Chinese posters do not have individual names on them and are seen as a communal expression of social ideals. This is very different than the individualism of western art.

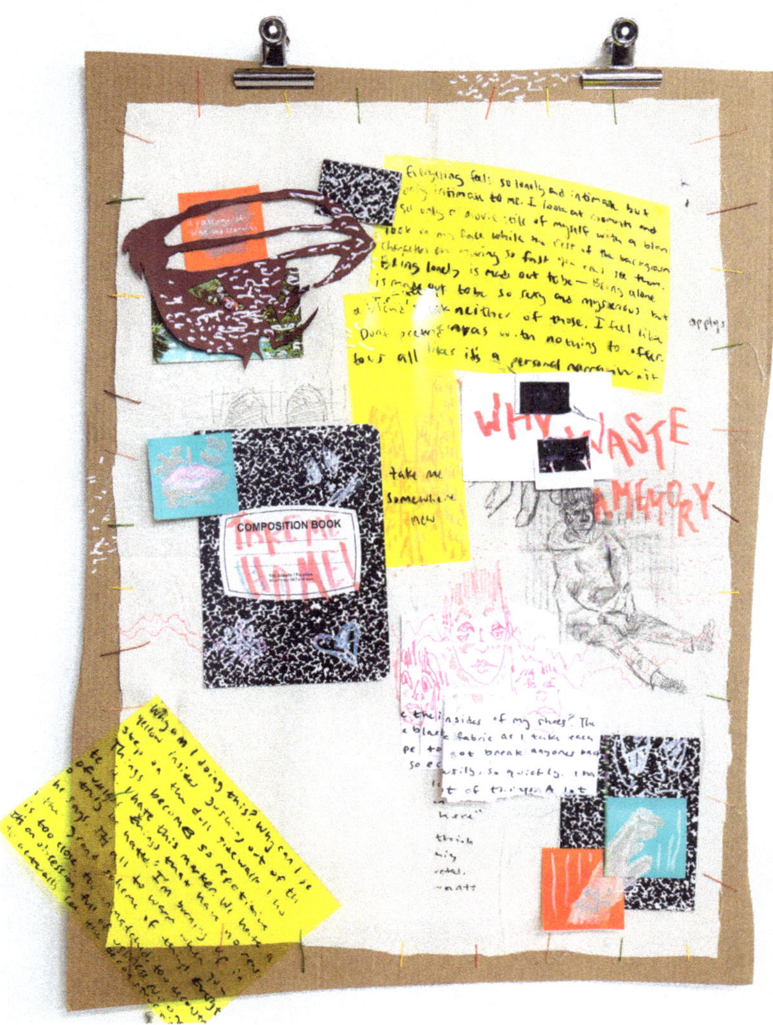

Noah Anthony

Assignment 5: Veterans Writing Team of Kansas City

We invite in a group of Veterans of Foreign Wars, men and women who have fought in Vietnam, Iraqi, Afghanistan, and other continuing conflicts. They discuss their experiences and the students are then given poems and short prose writings by the Veterans. The students then are asked to make a broadside concerning the writing. Create an image with text that opens up and reflect the power of the Vet's writings. The above assignments working with Russian Constructivism and Chinese Cultural Posters the student is working from modes of graphic communication. In other assignments the students are asked to work from their own internal story, from their memory. Use image/text to communicate their own experience. With the Vets they are working from someone's direct experience. They meet the person, see their emotions and feelings in their reading and in their face. The source of the communication is known and direct, not historical or secondary through a book or media reality. They produce broadsides or posters combining handmade scanned information and use Photoshop and image research to develop the content for the piece. This assignment is only an introduction to helping an external community communicate and be understood. It is also a discussion of listening, clients and collaboration. In the spring semester I teach a 5-week Image text and creative writing course. This introduction to design as social practice is more deeply investigated in that workshop.

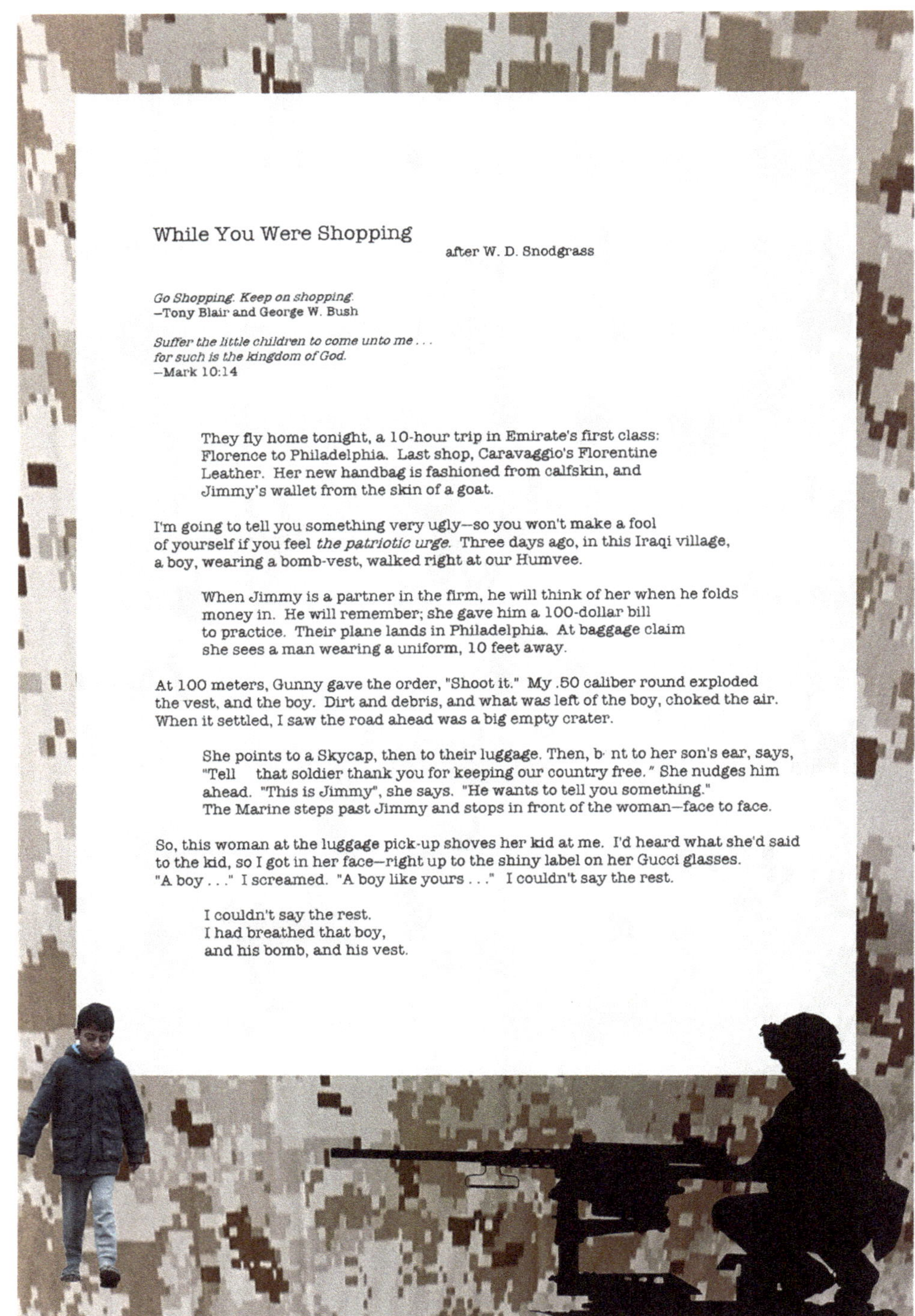

H.C. Palmer Kansas City Veterans writing Team collaboration

Assignment 6: Final Assignment

Make a poster or information graphic (Edward Tufti) using information concerning your life and your experience. Use the range of assignments you have encountered in the Visual Forces workshop. Such as the use of silhouettes, black and white engraved language, your experiences with Russian Constructivism, Cultural Revolution posters, The Veterans Writing Team, the stamp project and others to produce this graphic. The work is to be digitally printed as a 30X22 Inkjet archival print, on the paper of your choosing. The piece can combine printing and direct hand work on the paper. The hand developed pieces can be scanned or Photograph and reworked as a digital file or be added to the paper after the printing is completed.

This assignment allows them to reconsider their studio exercises and experiences. It allows them to draw on their cultural research, technical and visual literacy experiences. and it allows them to work from deeply held personal knowledge and use that knowledge to best develop their own expression. It allows them to express personal concerns and social and cultural issues tied to their individuation. Lastly it lets them select to work directly from drawing and collage and the "hand" or work solely in a digital mode or a combination of the two.

Thoughts on developing the final project for a section of educational outcomes:

Each final project for a set of assignments goes back over what we have learned and extends the assignment providing the student greater self-expressive and content opportunities. Some assignments are for learning and expanding the students base of skills and knowledge leading to a final assignment where they conceptually have more breadth. This process moves from first being focused on technical and formal issues to issues of content and personal vision.

Color Design Essentials

Color may be divided into two areas theoretical and practical. Color theory is an attempt to explain the nature of color related to how the eye determines a color and its value. Understanding how light reflected off a surface produces the visual effect of seeing a color. It is the realization that no object is a certain color. Color is in constant change, effected by the change in the quality of light, the association of proximity to other colors and other factors. All colors disappear at night leaving only tints of grey and black.

For the designer and artist, the focus is on understanding colors practical visual effects. This begins with a strong understanding of the basic grammar of color and then using color experientially to comprehend it in an intuitive and spontaneous manner. To achieve a spontaneous and knowledgeable use of color takes time and repetition.

In teaching color the emphasis is first on learning the grammar of color including understanding the color wheel and the glossary of terms that describe color professionally. Practical color methods and vocabulary are well established and easily learnable. They are essential as an under penning to move to the level of intuitive use of color. In themselves this practical information will not make a student more sensitive to using color. That sensitivity comes from using color, and experiencing its effects. True sensitivity comes with years of using color not in a week-long session of color study. I realize that by giving future assignments that use color as components helps provided the depth of experience needed to understand color intuitively. But first I want to make sure that the students have a grasp of the grammar of color.

There are many ways to approach the study of color. The exercises presented here are based on Johannnes Itten's treatise on color systems based on his book the Art of Color.

Content for Color Study:

Primary colors, secondary colors and tertiary colors, complementary colors, chroma, intensity, saturation, luminance, value, contrast, tint, shade, hue
Monochromatic, analogous, warm and cool, harmony, active and passive, color wheel
subtractive color and additive color
Color Systems: CMYK, RGB, Pantone
Itten's color contrasts
proportion, dominant, subdominant and accent

I provide a lecture on the scientists and artists that have shaped our understanding and vocabulary concerning color. I have the students watch the YouTube video *Goethe's Theory of Colors*. He points out that colors in physics can be measured but colors carry a deeper cultural set of mystical impressions. Colors produce feelings, they give us emotional energy. *Goethe's Theory of Color* provides the students with an interesting introduction to color theory and how light changes our perception of color.

The student's look up and become acquainted with:

J. Itten
Joseph Albers
Albert Musell
Johann Wolfgang von Goethe,
Wassily Kandinsky

Michel Eugène Chevreul.
Charles Newton
Matisse and the Fauvist

Learning Vocabulary Through Color Exercises in Photoshop.

To achieve a practical understanding of color vocabulary and to explore the meanings of those terms through studio practice we use *Color waqux,* an on line site dedicated to Johannes Itten's color studies. We follow the outline and progression of the web site and the students are asked to study and learn the properties of color as they are laid out by J. Itten. They are given written test questions and asked to use the site to answer the questions and then are retested until each student gets all the questions correct.

We further use Photoshop to explore through a studio experience the deeper meanings of the vocabulary and color concepts. Photoshop is a great tool for studying color because there is no mixing and drying time. If a color is produced that is incorrect it can be changed with amazing quickness. We do color exercises in Photoshop to create value charts, and explore terms such as saturation, value, intensity, hue, chroma, tint, and shade. This can be done with great efficiency, and work can easily be checked and the exercise repeated till each student gets the correct answers.

For example the students are given an exercises to produce a chart with 10 warm values of a hue with moderate intensity. They go to the color picker in Photoshop move the cursor to a warm color select one then move the cursor to the mid-range of the field of color displayed and select a mid-range tone. Then copy that tone into their color chart. They then repeat the process 10 times selecting 10 warm moderate hues of equal value. This exercise quickly confirms saturation, value, and hue. They are now prepared to use these terms in more complex assignments using collage and mix color.

These lectures and exercises lead to the student understanding the terms and more importantly the concepts behind the terms with amazing efficiency. The goal of the color study is to have the students learn the terms and their physical properties through exercises that were first covered in the Itten colorworqx web program.

To deepen the understanding of what they have experienced we then do a series of Photoshop works based on Itten color contrasts. The students are asked to photograph architectural structures. The Photographs are taken into Photoshop and simplified as posterized images that reduce the complexity of the 3d forms to flat 2d shapes. The student is then instructed to use Itten contrasts fill in the color shapes in the posterized image. We use the same abstract pattern to go through all of Itten's contrasts. Choosing the architecture shows investigate how a 3d form can be transformed into a 2D series of flat patterns and color relationships. The posterized 3D form provides an abstraction with no representational content. This image allows the student to work on color relationships and not be concerned with content expression or meaning. It allows us to focus on the quality and relations between the colors and discuss the meaning of the Itten color contrasts. The works produced are purposely small in scale 6x8 inches and are printed as inkjet prints. There are 7 Itten contrast and each student creates work related to each one.

We now cut and tear up our inkjet prints and make a complex collage of the parts. This image is gridded off and scaled up onto a large sheet of archival paper 22x30 inches. The students then mix colors to match the printed colors. The review of these paintings allows us to discuss the difference in quality between digital images viewed on the computer, printed images and painting. We end these exercises in color study by having the students determine their own set of color contrasts and make a series of works. abstract painting must follow pre-mixed color and there is not any brush mixing on the surface of the paper. The final critique covers the qualities of color and how well they work together. We also compare the works to music and try to describe their emotional value.

The last exercise is a color test that ask them to define all basic color terms historical figures and other ideas related to color such as color systems. In the end we have only begun to touch on understanding color and there are many excellent exercises to deepen the students color experience and knowledge. With as much content that needs to be covered in Foundation, depth is difficult to achieve. More importantly the goal is to have the student equipped with a sound introduction to build on in future assignments and in their own studio.

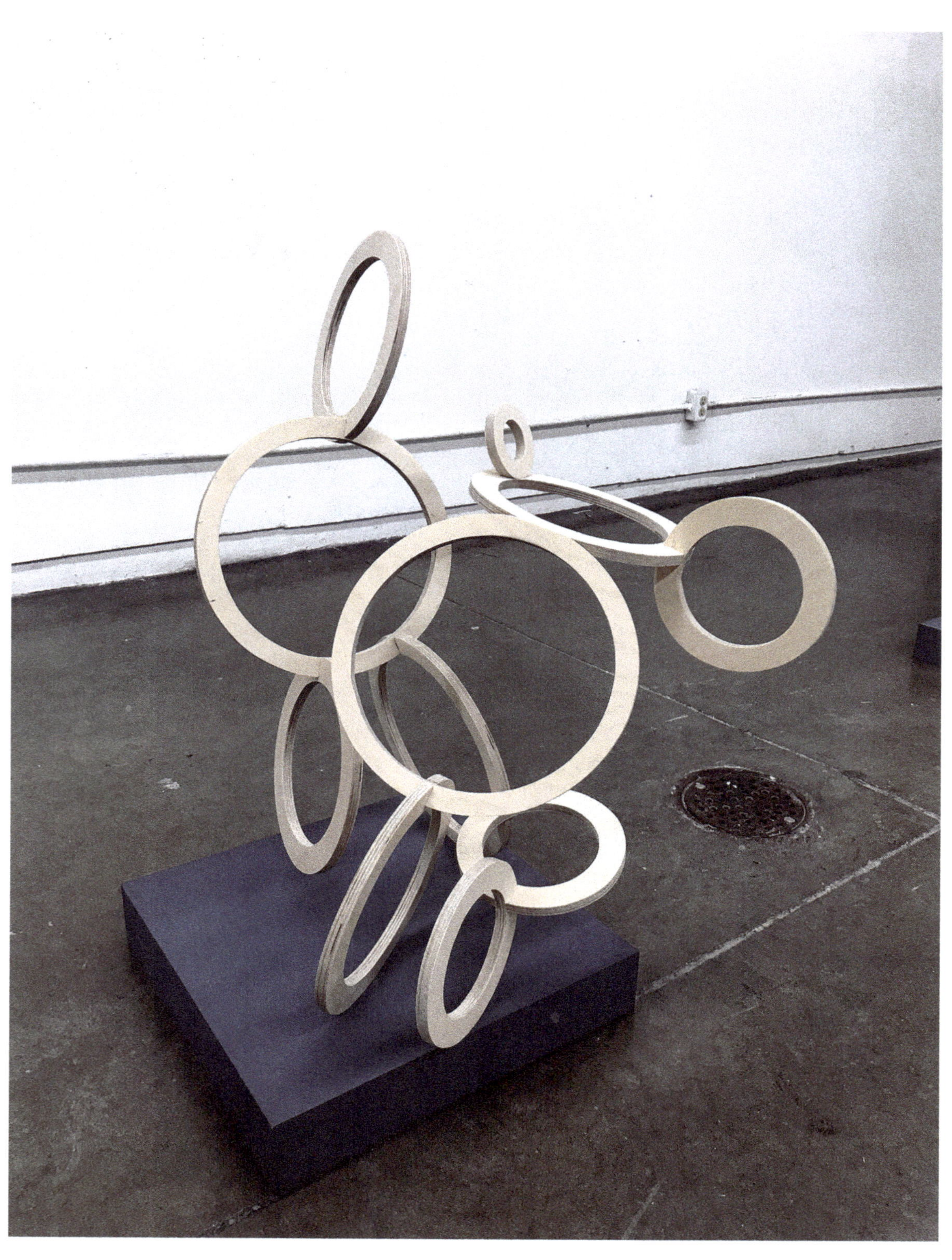

3D Structural Abstraction is a series of assignments and experiences to help the students understand 3-dimensional design elements and principals, and analyze the outcomes. This section of study sets up core visual literacy and 3 D design concepts, working processes and a language for describing and working with 3D formal elements in a knowledgeable manner.

I divide the 3-dimensional investigations into three areas: Geometric form building, based on modernist sculptural and architecture; personal narrative; and organic growth and movement. These concepts are touched on throughout the semester in investigations of perception and visual forces and then in depth during the focus of 3-dimensional forms in structural abstraction.

In perception and visual forces 3-dimensional assignments are introduced and are part of the overall learning outcomes. For example, when we are working with abstract drawing, line and gesture we make 3-dimensional drawings in the studio using bamboo shade slats, clips, hot glue and wire. The bamboo slats are 5 foot wide by ¾ inch. They easily bend and a ring can be produced with hot glue or clips to hold the form in place. These forms are related to basket construction so we look at forms, cultures and structures that use this process for making architecture and baskets.

We look at forms from bird's nests, to Indian baskets from the Navajo and Hopi Nations, Martin Puyear's woven forms, to the bird's nest stadium designed by Jacques Herzog and Pierre de Meuron. From the student's sculptural works produced with the bamboo slats we do drawings and project shadows onto the studio walls to combine 3-dimensional and 2-dimensional forms into a single installation. Next, we photograph the sculptures and take them into Photoshop and explore the forms graphic possibilities and print a series of 12x18 laser print graphics.

Again, the studio assignment and use of materials is enriched by cultural investigation and a broader view of the history of the use of the woven basket forms. Often in the focus on visual forces we investigate collage and graphic images as 3-dimensional objects. We start with concertina folded forms. The students learn to make this simple book form and are asked to design graphics for both sides of the folded book. Since the sides are opposites we ask them to have one side represent their internal private world and one their external-self presented to society. We also use templates to make forms out of heavy paper of cars, houses, tents and other forms. The forms are set up in Photoshop so as to again be able to print graphic images on the outside and inside of the 3-dimensional form. We discuss the importance of conceptual opposites as content.

This area of study is supported by *Access to Tools Woodshop*, where the students learn to build a wooden structure using a variety of wood working tools such as the table, band saws and sanders. In the recent past we devised a project using plywood to make sculptural forms from wooden rings. We began to explore the use of rings for building forms using rings sizes 12 inch to 4 inch diameters. Prior to cutting the plywood rings we use a band saw to cut laminated corrugated cardboard into the various sized rings. These forms were then used as forms for the construction of towers, horizontal works, spherical and other forms. The cardboard work allows for relatively quick exploration of the possibilities of varying 3-dimensional combinations. Like the bamboo 3-dimensional spacial drawings we design rings sculptures to be suspended and others to be attached to a 20x20 inch base.

The rings are by their nature a linear element and the sculptures take advantage of this quality. By cutting the rings into fourths or halves the student's make curved lines and complex linear shapes. Joining the curved elements together provided the student with linear works where the focus is on being viewed primarily from two sides. These linear forms seem to only have a front and the back. We discuss this problem and other possibilities, do the sculptures have an interior and an exterior? Can a two-sided piece be made more interesting by curving the linear form to provide a more complex linear form? When does the curved linear form attain a front and back side and internal and external visual quality?

The final ring assignment ask the students to use the provided material to make a highly crafted plywood ring sculpture based on the designed possibilities experienced during the cardboard ring constructions. This project takes the students through the use of the wood studio and all the major tools such as the band saw, table saw, and sanders.

Again, we move with fluidity between 3-dimensional and 2-dimensional investigations by photographing the sculptures and cutting the sculptural images out from the background then the students are asked to think about where they would place the sculptures virtually on the grounds of the Nelson Atkins Museum of Art. This exercise brings up important discussion on placement of sculptural forms in community and how the forms best reside in relation to open green space and architecture. They end by making digital laser jet prints of the virtual sculptures on the museum grounds.

For research we cover a good deal of ground looking and investigating images of contemporary sculpture and architecture. These architects and artist do not always directly relate to the assignment as Martin Puryear does to the basket project. The broader investigation is to make the students aware of possibilities and build a more substantial grounding in 3-dimensional forms.

We go to the computer lab and have the students look up and research artists such as Brancusi, Henry Moore, David Smith, Ludwig Mies van der Rohe, Saha Hadid, Louise Bourgeois, Frank Lloyd Wright, Ursula von Rydingvard, Frank Gehry, Willie Cole, and others. Many of these artists can be seen in Kansas City at the Nelson Atkins Museum.

We also explore work rooted in narrative and personal/social storytelling looking at Kiki Smith, Renee Stout, James Luna, Magdalena Abakanowicz, and Betye Saar. The students are assigned to create a narrative sculpture from an object such as a ladder, suitcase, large bound book(s) chair, book shelf or container. They work form scanning in family photographs, letters, souvenirs, old photographs or commercials and other ephemera. The object, let's say a char is not simply painted but can be cut into parts and reassembled, then sanded, painted and collaged to make the final work.

Very important to the 3-dimensional investigation is to move beyond geometric forms to organic forms based in nature. Forms created by erosion, topography, sand, wind, water and patterns of growth. So we investigate these possibilities by making topographical landscapes from laminated cardboard. Each student makes a piece that is 12x12 inches and we combine the 20 individual works into a single topographical work. Working as a collaborative team the students rework existing pieces and make new pieces to produce a continuous flowing topographical form.

We also use plaster to stiffen cloth. The cloth folds have a similarity to sand and water forms. We investigate the forms from the harden cloth with cardboard, nails, wire, or wooden skewers. We are using hard materials to simulate organic forms. Again, we photograph and draw from the works and explore their graphic possibilities.

Concepts we investigate: Detachment, touching, overlapping, interpenetration, union, subtraction, intersection, coinciding, tension and compression, visual distribution, similarity, shape gradation, union or subtraction, path of graduation (morphing), speed and direction, gravity, position, frame of reference, environmental placement.

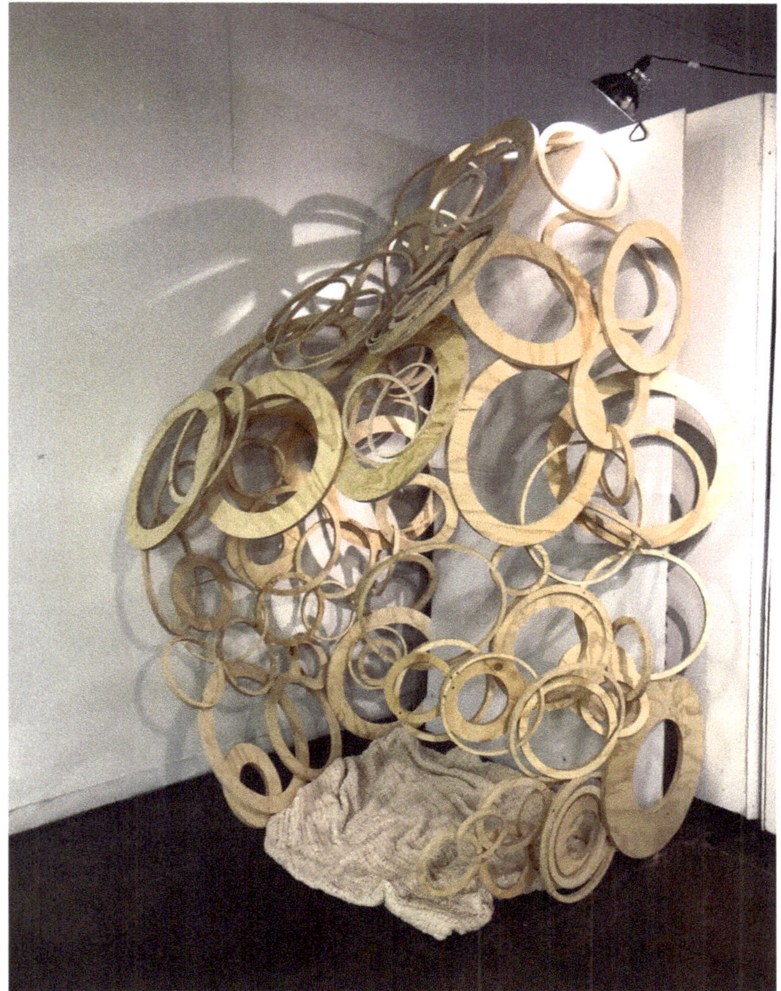

Bri Armstrong

Other content in the past has included explorations of:

- Assemblage structures and bass relief seen vertically hung on a wall
- Topographical structures to be viewed as horizontal structures viewed on a table
- Towers built using architectural building elements
- Free flowing 3d designs based on wind and water flowing natural forms
- Geometric and curve linear sculptures
- Deconstruction and reconstruction of objects such as suitcases or shoes
- Creation of sculpture forms using dressmaking patterns to produce large paper forms
- Explorations of topography and texture using cardboard, plaster and slip
- Construction of geometric models from paper templates, these forms are used to create more complex sculptures
- Use of flexible materials to create organic processes such as flowing water
- Creation of curved linear sculptures using a variety of materials including plastic, cardboard and or thin sheets of metal
- Investigation of tensile strength and stretch materials
- Investigation of architectural structures using wooded skewers as building material
- Building life size shelters from found materials
- Use of long thin wood scraps and plastic ties to create large scale woven structures
- Creation of puppets and marionettes
- Interrelationships of 3D form

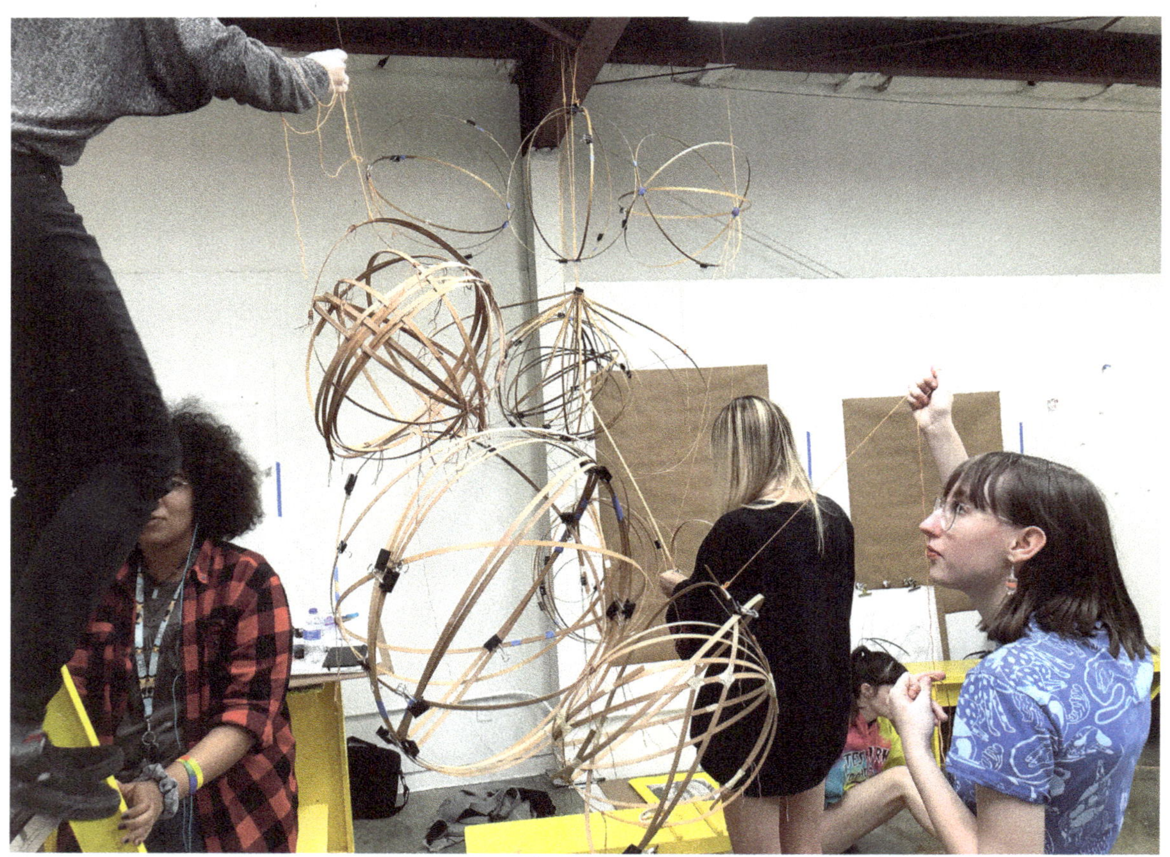

Students collaborate on installation of ring bamboo forms

Final projects

Final assignment for the year:

At mid-semester and again in the final 2 weeks of the studio, the course reaches a momentary conclusion. A moment when sets of concepts, processes and experiences have been well established. At this point it is time to determine what the students have learned by having them use their creative experiences to formulate their own assignment. The students are given the following outline on which to construct their final assignment.

Lateral thinking: come up with three possible projects that all use a variety of forms of studio investigation such as digital, drawing and sculptural components. Which is the primary investigation and which is supportive? We will discuss these in studio as a community and then begin to write up your final proposal.

- Describe the studio project you are interested in completing.
- Which of the assignments and experiences is your studio project related to and how?
- What will be the artistic and cultural research that extends and supports the studio project?
- What are the materials you will use and how will the work be presented?
- Describe how you will use your studio time (a minimum of 24 hours work) to research, investigate and produce the project. If work is to be printed, plan on when it needs to go to the central print studio for production)
- What is the cost of the project?
- Keep a studio working journal of your thoughts, unexpected changes, variations, new possibilities and other changes to the project.
- Prepare a presentation for the studio to explain the concept of your project, changes from the original concept that occurred, success and difficulties, things you would do different if starting over, list of new alternative ideas opportunities and variation from your journal.
- Document the piece as a raw photo file and correct the image as needed.

The students have not been allowed to do what they want based on self-expression but have to work from the range of assignments they have experienced over the semester. For the mid-term and final assignments they are given the freedom to conceptualize their own studio project but it must be based on what we have done over the semester. They are not allowed to go backwards to what they may have done prior to KCAI. They can use the skills that most interest them but they have to use them within the context of what they have experienced in the semester. They must include cultural research to support their studio work and must chart the development of their journey.

These "final" assignments are in reality a test to see what the students have learned, do they understand creative lateral thinking, have they accomplished the focus and commitment to work beyond their tolerance as needed. Can they conceptualize their own studio project or are they still dependent on the faculty to provide the concept and they remain good worker bees. The most important skill that a student leaving Foundation takes to the upper division is not technical, or studio rigor, but is conceptual. Do they know how to work independently in studio? It does not matter if they go to painting or fiber if they can conceptualize and research, set a direction of studio investigation for themselves they will learn and work productively in their majors. Of course, in the end all of these skills technical, conceptual and ability to work are equally important to success in and after school.

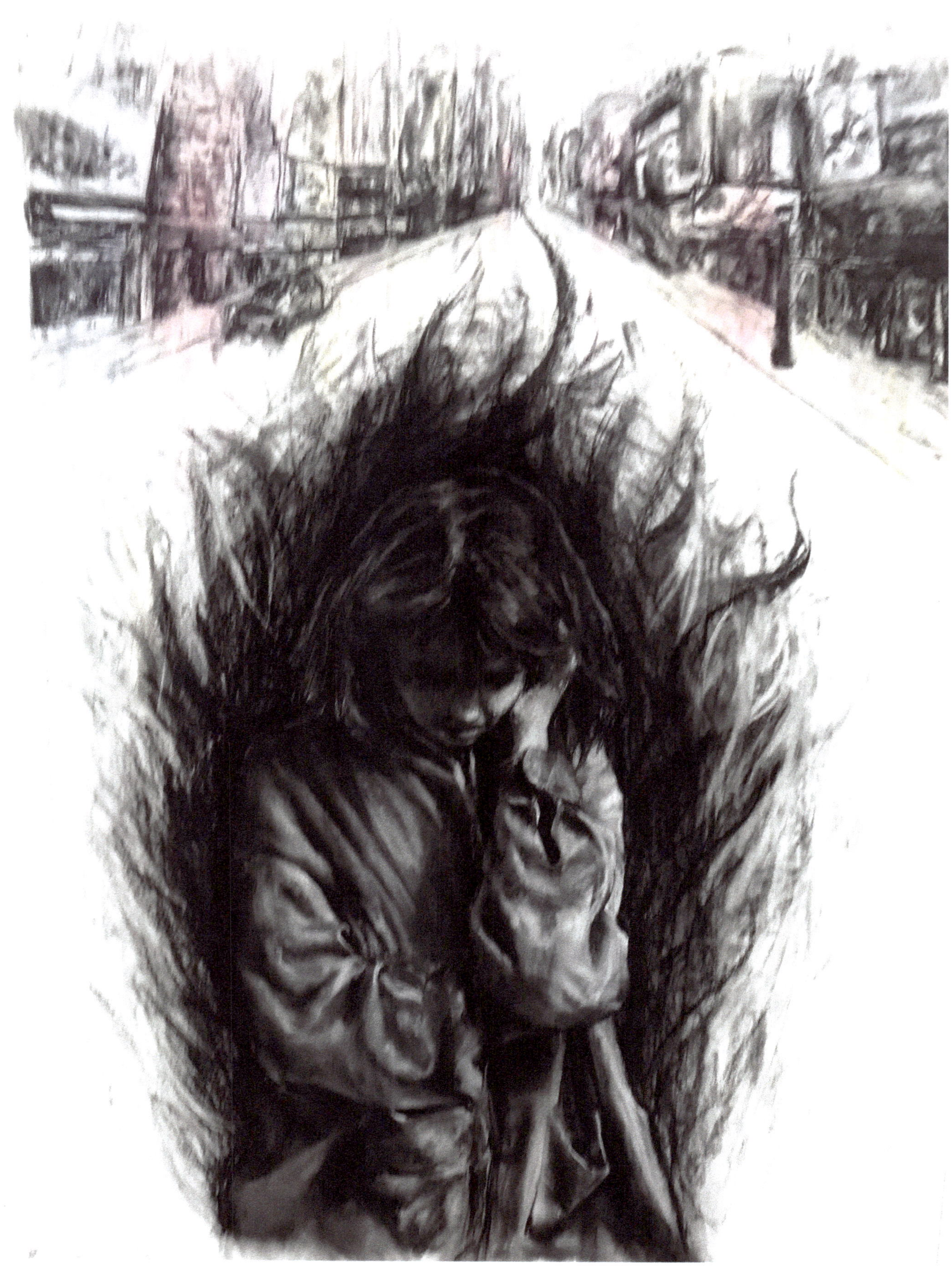

Daisy Sieben

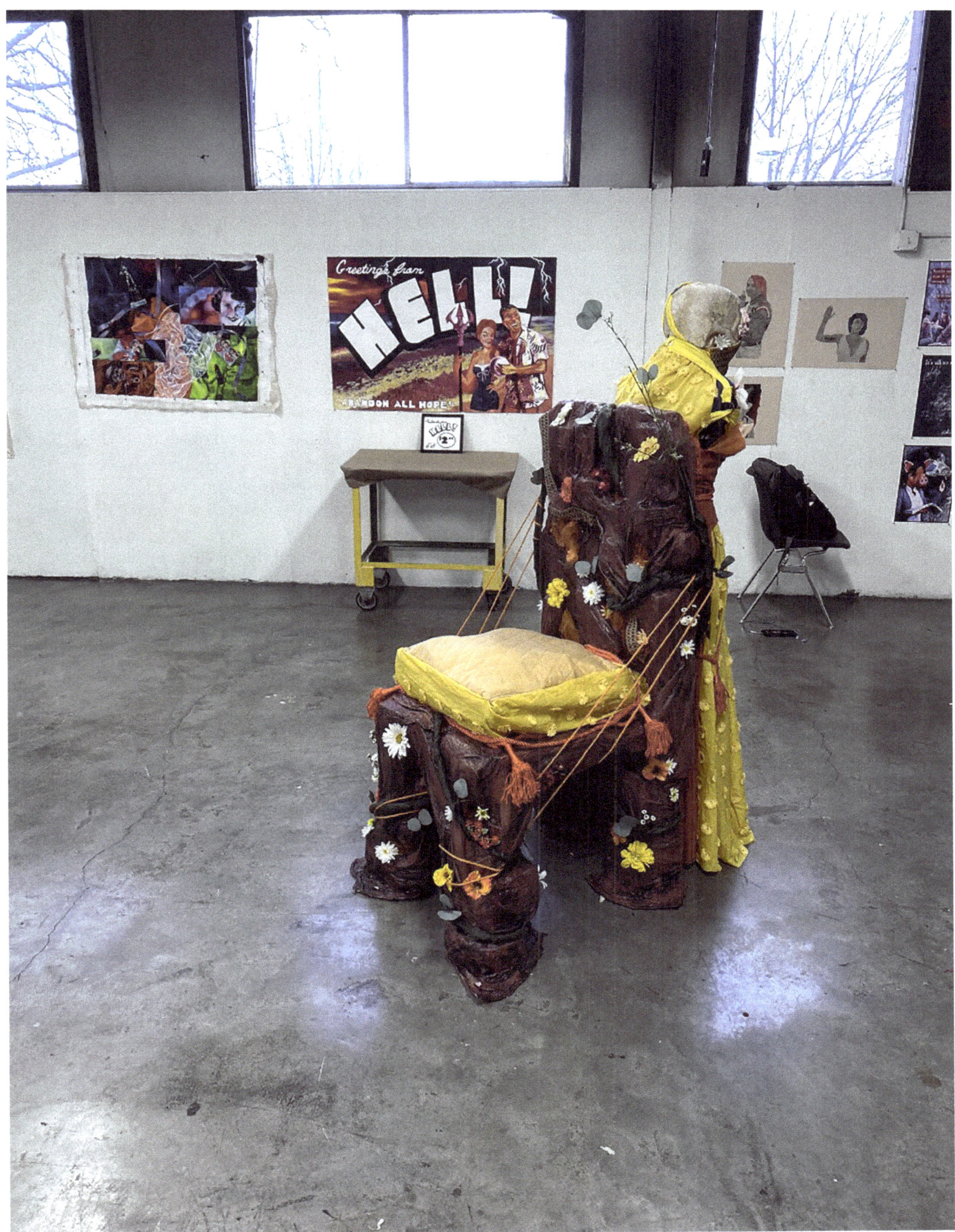

Final Exhibition

Evaluation

Mid-term and end of the year:

Evaluation in my Foundation sessions are NOT based on talent and or the manifest quality of the work produced. The expectation guiding your evaluation centers on your learning, i.e. your demonstration that you are going beyond the primary knowledge you brought with you to the program. Our goal is not self-expression or doing what we want based on what we know. We seek not to simply expand our talents, interests and technical know-how. Instead Foundation asks you to grow creatively, intellectually and professionally. You will be evaluated on your ability to:

- Move beyond your primary understanding of the assignment through research discussion studio exploration critical and creative thinking
- Go beyond your first attempt using exploration of materials making and remaking, a high tolerance for hard work and the ability to play with focus and intensity.
- Connect your expression and ideas to layers of content including contemporary art and design, history, science, social/political streams of thought, popular culture, technology and other areas of content.
- Decode, describe and be critical about visual art including works from assignments, contemporary works, popular culture and history.
- Have a high degree of craft, concern for quality, interaction of visual relationships and processes.
- Use professional terminology in describing, reviewing critiquing, discussing visual art poetry and assignments
- Learn on your own, do not wait for the instructor to fill all the gaps. Learn to be self-motivated and productive
- Be a positive member of the community: This is a very important part of your professional life and will be developed by successful collaboration with all members

What does the future hold for Foundation and education of the next generation of artists?

On the horizon are new concerns that will change the traditional scope of teaching visual literacy and discipline-based content. New content driven by social change sustainability, concern for cultural respect, technical innovation and ecological pressures will change the way we think about art and will change the way we need to teach young artists. I have written a book titled *Shared Visions* on social practice as a guide for instruction and defining the territory. Yet little of this content is used in my Foundation instruction in the first semester. The department sees the importance of sustainability, ecology and social practice in art instruction but has not as yet developed a systemic or dynamic approach for enclosing it deeply in the curriculum. The habitual and entrenched history of departmental education and old tested approaches prevent a reinvention of developing programs and curriculum that is non-disciplinary and experimental. This is a problem for many institutions and will not be easily solved. Here in the KCAI Foundation Department in the second semester each faculty teaches 3, five-week sessions. In this structure we are able to include this new and dynamic content in very inventive ways. Invite in faculty for a single session to teach community-based curriculum, or a course based in ecological or sustainable concepts. Yet this is not the major re-invention of the present system. It is an exciting time to be a faculty and search for a bridge between Andy Goldsworthy and Kara Walker, Ai Wei Wei and Judith Baca. These artists do not easily fit into the traditional disciplinary mode------------- and the future?

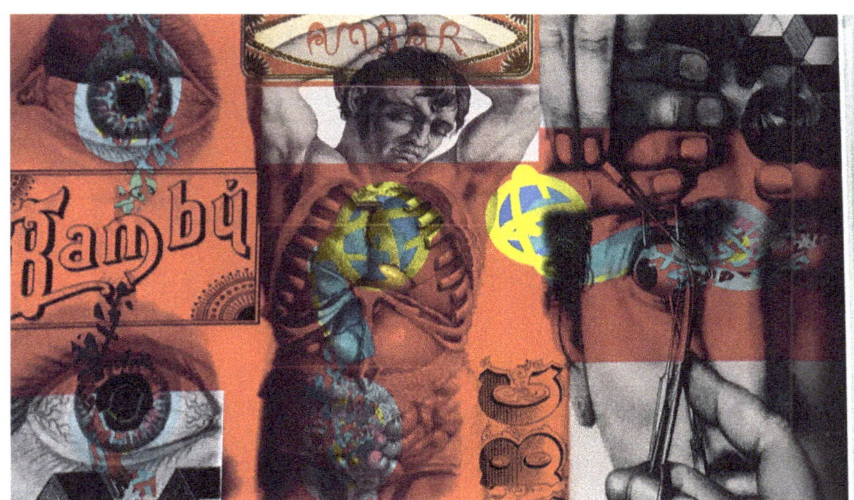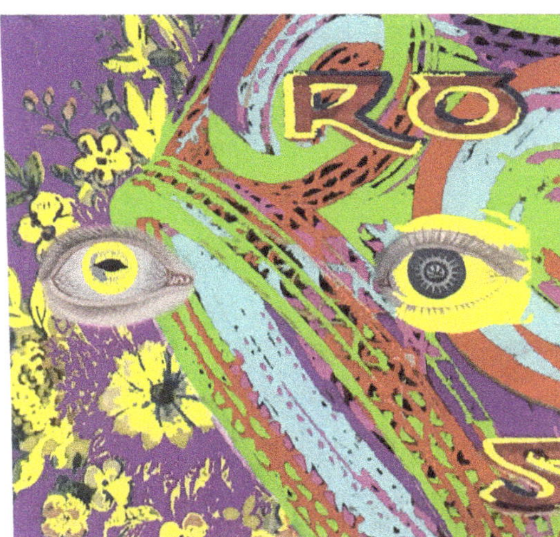

final exhibition

A last thought

Who need to read this book? Foundation faculty in a variety of teaching platforms from University settings to arts and craft residencies such as Penland School of Crafts. I believe there are thoughts experiences and ideas for all who are educators both in teaching art, creativity and well, just teaching. Now more than ever the United States needs independent thinkers that do not accept the given from Fox news or the reigning politicians. We need creative young people that can see the truth and react to it in creative ways finding novel solutions. So I guess this book is for all or at least many from students, to faculty or just those interested. Enjoy! --Hugh Merrill

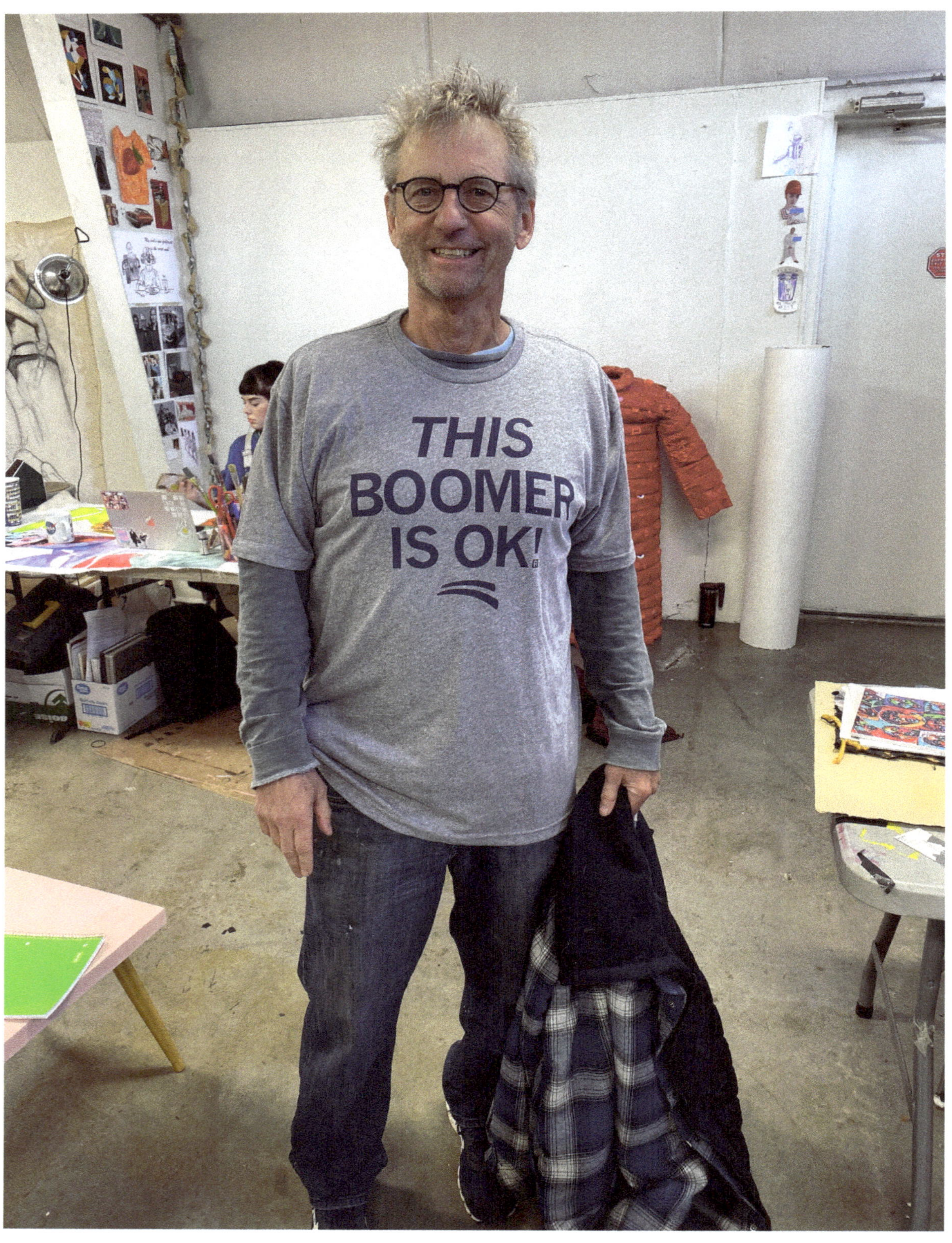